Choosing a New Organization for Management and Disposition of Commercial and Defense High-Level Radioactive Materials

Lynn E. Davis, Debra Knopman, Michael D. Greenberg, Laurel E. Miller, Abby Doll

With Paul Steinberg, Bruce R. Nardulli, Tom LaTourrette, Noreen Clancy, Zhimin Mao

Prepared for the U.S. Department of Energy

Environment, Energy, and Economic Development

A RAND INFRASTRUCTURE, SAFETY, AND ENVIRONMENT PROGRAM

This research was sponsored by the U.S. Department of Energy and was conducted in the Environment, Energy, and Economic Development Program within RAND Infrastructure, Safety, and Environment, a division of the RAND Corporation.

Library of Congress Cataloging-in-Publication Data is available for this publication.
ISBN: 978-0-8330-7640-3

The RAND Corporation is a nonprofit institution that helps improve policy and decisionmaking through research and analysis. RAND's publications do not necessarily reflect the opinions of its research clients and sponsors.
RAND® is a registered trademark.

Published 2012 by the RAND Corporation
1776 Main Street, P.O. Box 2138, Santa Monica, CA 90407-2138
1200 South Hayes Street, Arlington, VA 22202-5050
4570 Fifth Avenue, Suite 600, Pittsburgh, PA 15213-2665
RAND URL: http://www.rand.org/
To order RAND documents or to obtain additional information, contact
Distribution Services: Telephone: (310) 451-7002;
Fax: (310) 451-6915; Email: order@rand.org

Preface

Following the President's decision in January 2010 to withdraw the license application for a geologic repository at Yucca Mountain, Nevada, the Secretary of Energy established the Blue Ribbon Commission on America's Nuclear Future (BRC) to consider alternatives to the nation's current institutional arrangements for management and disposition of used fuel and defense high-level nuclear waste. In February 2012, the BRC issued its final report.[1] Among its recommendations was a call for a new, single-purpose organization to be established to replace the Office of Civilian Radioactive Waste Management (OCRWM) in the U.S. Department of Energy (DOE) that had been established under the authority of the 1982 Nuclear Waste Policy Act.[2]

The BRC suggested that a congressionally chartered federal corporation offers the most promising model, but the commission left open the possibility of alternative concepts to achieve the desired ends. In response to this recommendation, DOE asked the RAND Corporation to examine alternative organizational models for such a new management and disposition organization (MDO). Our study supports the work of DOE's Office of Nuclear Energy and the Management and Disposition Working Group (MDWG) formed to consider implementation options and activities.

The RAND Environment, Energy, and Economic Development Program

This research was conducted in the Environment, Energy, and Economic Development Program (EEED) within RAND Infrastructure, Safety, and Environment (ISE). The mission of ISE is to improve the development, operation, use, and protection of society's essential physical assets and natural resources and to enhance the related social assets of safety and security of individuals in transit and in their workplaces and communities. The EEED research portfolio addresses environmental quality and regulation, energy resources and systems, water resources and systems, climate, natural haz-

---

[1]   BRC, 2012.

[2]   Pub. L. 97-425.

ards and disasters, and economic development—both domestically and internationally. EEED research is conducted for governments, foundations, and the private sector.

Questions or comments about this report should be sent to the project leaders, Debra Knopman (Debra_Knopman@rand.org) and Lynn Davis (Lynn_Davis@rand. org). Information about EEED is available online (http://www.rand.org/ise/environ. html). Inquiries about EEED projects should be sent to the following address:

Keith Crane, Director
Environment, Energy, and Economic Development Program, ISE
RAND Corporation
1200 South Hayes Street
Arlington, VA 22202-5050
703-413-1100, x5520
Keith_Crane@rand.org

Contents

Figures

Tables

Summary

Introduction

Finding ways to safely store and ultimately dispose of used fuel from commercial and defense reactors as well as high-level nuclear waste from defense and other operations has been on the national policy agenda for decades and remains a matter of considerable debate. At the request of the President, the Secretary of Energy convened the Blue Ribbon Commission on America's Nuclear Future (BRC) in 2010 "to conduct a comprehensive review of policies for managing the back end of the nuclear fuel cycle" and to recommend a new strategy.[3]

The BRC, among its many recommendations, called for the creation of an organization chartered by Congress and structured as a federal government corporation.[4] The U.S. Department of Energy (DOE) asked RAND to support its effort to respond to the recommendations of the BRC by looking at different organizational models for a new, single-purpose organization to manage and dispose of used fuel and high-level defense and other nuclear waste—a management and disposition organization, hereafter referred to as an MDO.

Looking Back

We first took a retrospective look to ask what the major problems were in nuclear waste management in the past decades and where responsibility for those problems lies. In so doing, we examined five areas: (1) governance and leadership, (2) funding and budget control, (3) the siting process, (4) procurement and personnel rules, and (5) the public trust. What we discovered was that the organizational design of the Office of Civilian Radioactive Waste Management (OCRWM) within DOE contributed less to the problems than the Nuclear Waste Policy Act (NWPA) itself and subsequent congressional and executive branch actions. These actions included most notably the 1987 amendments, which designated Yucca Mountain as the only candidate repository site, over

---

[3] DOE, 2010a.

[4] BRC, 2012, p. x.

the objections of Nevada, and changes in budgeting that severely restricted the Secretary of Energy's access to the Nuclear Waste Fund (NWF). In the light of OCRWM's history and the actions of Congress and various administrations as a whole, perhaps the most important lesson to be drawn is that organizational form may only have a limited effect on a program's performance; that is, a well-designed organization is a necessary but not sufficient condition for success. As flawed as OCRWM's program implementation may have been at times, it is difficult to imagine that any organization could have successfully executed the program in the absence of both public support in the affected state and sustained funding from Congress, itself an indicator of public support.

Organizational Models

We explored potential organizational models, paying specific attention to federal government corporations (GOVCORPs) but also to federally chartered private corporations (PRIVCORPs) and independent government agencies (IGAs). In Chapter Three, we describe their characteristics—in terms of such things as the charter, direct oversight, the role of the President and the White House, the role of Congress, funding, and personnel management, procurement, and contracting—and how they perform their specific missions. What we found was that the models involve different avenues for blending the features of a private-sector organization (e.g., independence and internal flexibility) and of a government agency (e.g., public trust, political oversight and accountability, and political influence). The key takeaway of this examination lies in the flexibility the U.S. government has in choosing among the different organizational models but also the specific characteristics of each of the models.

Analysis Framework

Although there could be reasons for picking one organizational model over another, we discovered that more analysis was required, with a focus on the critical attributes an organization needs to achieve its performance goals and carry out its responsibilities. Using our analysis framework, we defined the key *responsibilities* of a new MDO that derive from its mission, its organizational *performance goals*, the *critical organizational attributes* needed to meet those performance goals, and the various *structural and procedural features* necessary to perform those critical attributes. See Figure S.1.

Next, we matched the structural and performance features with each of the organizational models (PRIVCORP, GOVCORP, and IGA) to determine which of these were present or could be built in to each model. From this analysis, we came to the view that several critical attributes are weaker in or missing from the PRIVCORP

Figure S.1
Framework for Linking Responsibilities, Performance Goals, Attributes, and Features

RAND *MG1230-S.1*

model, including public accountability, public interest mission, and linkages to the executive branch and Congress that would ensure the political credibility and influence needed for siting. (Indeed, independence from the President and Congress is a primary rationale for a PRIVCORP.) Although these features could theoretically be written into a PRIVCORP's charter, achieving these would be prohibitively difficult for a U.S. private corporation whose primary loyalty is to its stockholders in earning a profit. However, the critical attributes exist or can be built into the two other organizational models, an IGA and a GOVCORP, given the many different variations in the characteristics that these organizations can take.

Designing a New MDO

In designing a new MDO, policymakers will need to go through a series of steps that will involve a number of choices, first about the relationship of the MDO to the President, next about Congress's role, third about the source of the MDO's funding, and then the role of stakeholders and other MDO organizational features. We begin with the President and Congress because their roles are critical in setting the tone and shaping the relationship among the MDO, stakeholders, and the public.

Step 1: The President's Role

The critical choice for policymakers is how the MDO should relate to the President, i.e., whether it should be a direct relationship, as in an IGA, or a relationship that is largely independent of the President, as in a GOVCORP. See Figure S.2.

- **Direct relationship:** Reporting directly to the President, as with an IGA, ensures that the public interest is taken into account in all the operations of the MDO. The influence residing with the President would be available to achieve the siting of the storage and disposal facilities, and the executive branch would be able to influence MDO operations in ways to make certain that the siting tasks are being accomplished; the storage, transport, and disposal of used fuel and nuclear waste

Figure S.2
The MDO's Relationship to the President

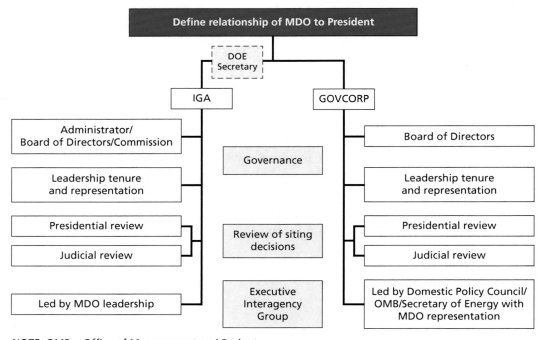

NOTE: OMB = Office of Management and Budget.
RAND *MG1230-S.2*

are being carried out safely; and situations do not arise in which a government bailout would be needed.

- **Independent relationship:** Greater independence from the President, as is typically the case in a GOVCORP, insulates the activities of the MDO from the turnover of administrations, provides the authority necessary to make decisions on siting without political interference, and allows flexibility in siting negotiations, operations (including contracting and procurement), and personnel policy.

In the case of an IGA, policymakers would have the choice of whether the MDO would report to the President directly or through the Secretary of Energy, as is the case today with Bonneville Power Administration (BPA). This would be different from the past when OCRWM was an office inside DOE. Reporting through the Secretary of Energy would be a way for MDO activities to continue to be closely integrated with other DOE-related activities. The case for having the MDO report directly to the President rests largely on the need to make a break from past problems associated with DOE's management of used fuel and defense high-level nuclear waste.

Having chosen either an IGA or a GOVCORP, policymakers will have some flexibility to build into the organization features to enhance its prospects of achieving its performance goals and lessen some of the potential disadvantages associated with the organizational form chosen. They would do this by making decisions with respect to each of the boxes in Figure S.2.

Independent Government Agency

If an IGA is preferred, policymakers would first need to choose its supervisory structure, i.e., whether the agency would be led by a governing board (e.g., the Federal Reserve), a commission (e.g., Nuclear Regulatory Commission [NRC]), or a single administrator (e.g., BPA, National Aeronautics and Space Administration [NASA]). While maintaining accountability, steps could then be taken to shape the governance of an IGA to achieve some degree of political insulation, e.g., by mandating a balance among political affiliations for a multimember board or commission. To further build political insulation and organizational stability, policymakers could preclude presidential review of the MDO's major decisions. The IGA administrator or board/commission chairman could also be designated to lead an interagency group to ensure the political credibility and influence necessary to carry out the MDO's responsibilities, particularly in siting.

Government Corporation

To increase the accountability of the leadership in a GOVCORP, policymakers could require in the legislative charter that the President nominate the members of the MDO's board of directors and mandate that their terms be relatively short and subject to periodic renewal. In addition to defining what experience and expertise they wished to have on the board, policymakers could designate a member of the executive branch to serve on the board. As a GOVCORP is designed to be insulated from presidential involvement, policymakers could make provision for some presidential role and review of the MDO's major decisions.

To tap into the resources of the federal government for providing the incentives that will be necessary to achieve the siting of the facilities and to gain influence over the activities of the executive branch agencies, including the regulators, policymakers could set up, under the Domestic Policy Council, Office of Management and Budget, or the Secretary of Energy, an ad hoc group with representation from executive departments, the regulatory agencies, and the GOVCORP leadership.

Step 2: Congress's Role

Policymakers will also need to address the relationship of the MDO to Congress and focus on oversight and the congressional role in decisions on siting. These will be independent of which organizational model is chosen. See Figure S.3.

Policymakers will need to decide whether the Senate will have a role in confirming the leadership of the MDO: the board of directors, commission, or agency administrator. If there is a role in confirmation, the Senate will need to put in place processes to avoid delays that could leave the MDO without the leadership it needs.

Figure S.3
The MDO's Relationship to the Congress and Funding Source

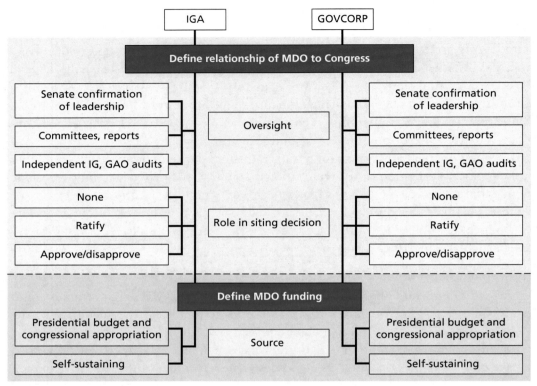

NOTE: IG = inspector general.
RAND *MG1230-S.3*

Policymakers will also need to make decisions as to which committees will exercise oversight over the operations and decisions of the MDO and through what types of testimonies and reports (on, for example, strategic plans, management and financial operations). To gain insight into the conduct of MDO activities, Congress could create an independent IG who is required to submit annual public reports and require audits by the GAO.

Finally, policymakers will need to decide whether Congress will be given any specific role in the various decisions that will be called for in the siting processes, i.e., the locations of the facilities and the agreements negotiated with states, tribes, and local communities. One possibility is for Congress to ratify these MDO decisions (e.g., as the Senate ratifies a treaty in an "up-down" vote); another possibility is that Congress approve or disapprove these decisions (e.g., as is done with the recommendations of the Base Closing and Realignment Commission to close military facilities).

History has shown that, under the terms and conditions of the NWPA, Congress fully involved itself in site selection, funding, and regulatory decisions and, in so doing, undermined public trust and confidence in the processes. Although Congress does have an important and constructive role to play in the future, there is an inherent tension between a consent-based siting approach and giving Congress the authority to veto agreements made between the MDO and consenting states, tribes, and local communities.

Step 3: MDO Funding

Perhaps the most important issue that policymakers will face is what will be the source of the MDO's funding, i.e., whether it will receive annual congressional appropriations or be able to fund its expenditures from operating revenues or other resources (i.e., "self-sustaining"). See Figure S.3. The decision on how the MDO is funded is independent of whether the organization is a GOVCORP or an IGA. The Tennessee Valley Authority (TVA) (a GOVCORP) has a dedicated funding stream; the NRC (an IGA) has a dedicated funding stream but is subject to an annual appropriation, and Amtrak (a GOVCORP) has both dedicated funding streams and annual appropriations. NASA (an IGA) receives annual appropriations.

In the case of annual appropriations, the Senate and House will be required to authorize and appropriate the funds, and the MDO will need to submit its budget through OMB and provide the supporting budget justification and documentation to the various congressional oversight committees. Even if funds are made available on a self-sustaining basis through a dedicated funding source, OMB and the Congress could still exercise oversight by requiring the MDO to submit quarterly and annual financial and management reports.

Step 4: Other Organizational Features

Whether an IGA or GOVCORP model is chosen, policymakers will need to define other features of a new MDO and include these in the enabling legislation: one is how the MDO will relate to its stakeholders, another is how it will be treated by federal and state regulatory agencies, a third is what responsibilities it will have for the management and disposition of both commercial and defense materials, and finally whether the MDO will be subject to federal personnel, procurement, and contracting rules. See Figure S.4.

Relationship to Stakeholders

The MDO will have multiple stakeholders (utility companies, states, local communities, tribes, nongovernmental organizations (NGOs) as well as the U.S. Department of Defense [DoD] and DOE), so policymakers will need to decide how these interests will be represented within the MDO itself or through different coordination and consultation mechanisms. One way is to call for their representation on a board of directors or commission. Another way is to set up advisory committees to gain advice and support with participation by some or all of these stakeholders.

Figure S.4
Other Organizational Features of the MDO

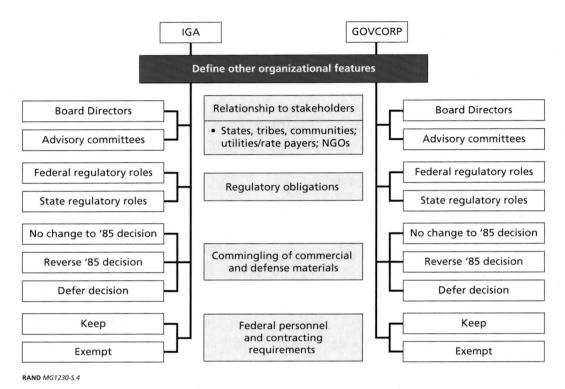

RAND *MG1230-S.4*

Regulatory Obligations and Liabilities

There are no choices for policymakers to make about federal environmental health and safety regulations, but there is a choice to be made regarding the regulatory role of states with respect to the sited facilities for protection of human health and the environment. Policymakers will also need to address the liability issues associated with the MDO's assumption of title to used fuel and nuclear waste, given the risks and costs tied to these materials.

Commingling of Commercial and Defense Materials

Policymakers will need to decide whether the MDO will be responsible for the management and disposition of both commercial and defense materials. An analysis of the choices (maintain the 1985 decision of commingled repository, reverse the 1985 decision and separate the repositories, or defer the decision) was outside the scope of this study.[5] If a decision is made to continue a policy of commingling, organizational

---

[5] For the 1985 decision, see Ronald Reagan, letter to Secretary of Energy John S. Herrington, "Disposal of Defense Waste in a Commercial Repository," Washington, D.C., April 30, 1985.

processes will be needed to manage the two funding streams in a unified manner, and this could be done for either an IGA or GOVCORP.

Federal Personnel, Procurement, and Contracting

An IGA would typically be bound by federal personnel rules and federal procurement and contracting requirements. To be able to attract the technical expertise and management talent as well as gain flexibility in hiring and firing, policymakers could exempt the new MDO from the personnel rules for some or all classes of employees. To provide flexibility for managing multiyear megaprojects, policymakers could provide flexibility to enable funding obligations for multi-year contracts, or could exempt the IGA from the federal procurement and contracting requirements.

Given that the rationale for forming a GOVCORP involves allowing the organization "to run on business-like principles," they often are exempted from at least some aspects of federal personnel management, procurement, and contracting requirements. Whether formed as an IGA or GOVCORP, policymakers will need to decide in its enabling legislation whether to exempt the MDO from these requirements (see Chapter Three).

Considerations Related to Choice of Organizational Form
Government Responsibility for Catastrophic Risk

In making a decision on the organizational form of a new MDO, policymakers will need to consider what role the U.S. government would play in situations in which major financial problems or other serious dangers arise. In an IGA, there would be no question that the government would have ultimate responsibility for any future risks (or catastrophic liability) that might arise in connection with managing used fuel and high-level waste. In contrast, a GOVCORP would not be backed by the full faith and credit of the U.S. government (unless Congress decided to make it so), and, at least in principle, the government would not necessarily be obligated to step in and bail out a GOVCORP (unless Congress specifies otherwise). Nevertheless, given the nature of the mission of managing used fuel, and the inherent and long-term risks that attach to this task, it is difficult to imagine that a difference would exist in practice: If a catastrophic risk event affecting large numbers of people and the environment were to occur, the U.S. government would be placed under tremendous pressure to take responsibility and to intervene to manage the risk.[6]

Evolution of the MDO as Its Roles Change Over Time

Given the varied responsibilities of the MDO and the time to accomplish its multiple tasks, policymakers will also need to consider whether an MDO should be created as a single fixed organization to carry out all its responsibilities over a long period of time or

---

[6]   See the response of the U.S. government to the BP oil spill (National Commission on the BP Deepwater Horizon Oil Spill and Offshore Drilling, 2011).

whether the MDO should be designed with characteristics that would change to meet the demands of different phases of its mission.

The argument for a fixed organization is that anticipated evolution of its organizational design could undermine the ability of the MDO to develop its own culture and management skills for carrying out its highly complex and multifaceted activities over the long term. Moreover, many of the MDO activities will need to be pursued simultaneously. On the other hand, the organizational culture and skills for achieving the siting of the consolidated storage and permanent disposal sites through a consent-based process will be very different from those required to successfully pursue a license application, construct multiple facilities, and then operate and close those facilities. When the organization is predominantly in its siting phase, it will require a skilled staff of negotiators, technical advisors, risk communicators, and individuals adept at public outreach. When the organization is predominantly in the phases of preparing a license application and planning construction, it will require individuals with sophisticated technical and project management skills teamed with strong public communicators.

One approach would be to choose a GOVCORP because of its inherent flexibility to hire and fire people easily, to change its own internal structure, and make decisions about when and how to contract out various tasks and functions. Another approach is to design the MDO to evolve by design, starting with an IGA, which embodies what will be needed to achieve consent-based siting: a close relationship to the President, public accountability, access to the resources of the federal government, and the ability to enter into long-term agreements. Depending on how they are led and managed, either a GOVCORP or IGA has the potential to achieve public trust.

Under either an IGA or GOVCORP, Congress could include a provision in the enabling legislation for periodic evaluations of organizational effectiveness, which could then provide the analytical basis for determining whether refinements or structural changes are warranted in the future. This is something akin to an adaptive management approach, embedded in the program now operating in Canada and Sweden, among others.[7] If the view is that the MDO may need to evolve in its organizational design, policymakers would need to address this in the enabling legislation. A transition could be provided within the structure of the enabling organization, or new legislation could be mandated.

Making the Choices

The success of any future MDO will be driven by many factors and unforeseen circumstances. The organizational form is only one of these factors: it is a necessary but not sufficient condition for success. Beyond the organization itself, the evolution of

---

[7]   Lee, 2003.

national priorities and changes in the political environment will have a profound effect on the success of any MDO in meeting the performance goals articulated by the BRC and outlined here. There is almost certainly more than one way to design a successful MDO. Still, it is likely the case that the more critical attributes are built into the organization, the better will be the chances of success.

What is needed is for policymakers to decide on these questions in a step-wise fashion, taking three key questions in turn:

1. What influence should the President have on the activities of the MDO to ensure the public interest and future success in the siting of the facilities while allowing the MDO the flexibility to carry out its responsibilities?
2. How insulated from and independent of congressional oversight should the MDO be while ensuring public accountability?
3. How should the MDO be structured (through board membership, advisory committees, or other mechanisms to involve stakeholders and the public) to increase the likelihood of instilling public trust and attracting interest, engagement, and commitment of states, tribes, and local communities in the siting of the facilities?

In answering these questions, policymakers will be striking a balance between the competing values of accountability and flexibility called for in the design of the new MDO.

Acknowledgments

We wish to express our gratitude to Phillip Niedzielski-Eichner, chair of the Management and Disposition Working Group (MDWG), and Christopher Hanson, chair of the MDWG Governance and Funding Integrated Task Team, for their support and guidance during the course of this study. We would also like to thank the many knowledgeable individuals who shared their valuable experience and perspectives with the RAND team, and especially Paul Light, who reviewed an earlier draft of this study. Finally, we are indebted to our RAND colleagues, who offered valuable critiques and guidance to us along the way. These include James Bartis, Frank Camm, Cynthia Cook, and Keith Crane. Lauren Bachman provided efficient and timely administrative support throughout the project. Lisa Bernard and James Torr thoroughly edited the document under a tight schedule and did so with great skill and patience.

Any errors or omissions are the responsibility of the authors.

Abbreviations

AMFM	Advisory Panel on Alternative Means of Financing and Managing Radioactive Waste Facilities
BPA	Bonneville Power Administration
BRC	Blue Ribbon Commission on America's Nuclear Future
CEO	chief executive officer
COMSAT	Communications Satellite Corporation
DoD	U.S. Department of Defense
DOE	U.S. Department of Energy
EEED	RAND Environment, Energy, and Economic Development
EPA	U.S. Environmental Protection Agency
FAA	Federal Aviation Administration
FAR	Federal Acquisition Regulation
FARS	Federal Acquisition Regulation System
FCRPS	Federal Columbia River Power Systems
FEDCORP	federal corporation for waste management
FERC	Federal Energy Regulatory Commission
FRA	Federal Railroad Administration
FTCA	Federal Tort Claims Act
GAO	U.S. Government Accountability Office (until 2004, the U.S. General Accounting Office)
GCCA	Government Corporation Control Act
GOVCORP	government corporation
GSE	government-sponsored entity
IAEA	International Atomic Energy Agency

ICC	Interstate Commerce Commission
IG	Inspector General
IGA	independent government agency
ISE	RAND Infrastructure, Safety, and Environment
M&O	management and operations
MDO	management and disposition organization
MDWG	Management and Disposition Working Group
MRS	monitored retrievable storage
NASA	National Aeronautics and Space Administration
NGO	nongovernmental organization
NRC	Nuclear Regulatory Commission
NWF	Nuclear Waste Fund
NWPA	Nuclear Waste Policy Act
NWTRB	U.S. Nuclear Waste Technical Review Board
OCRWM	Office of Civilian Radioactive Waste Management
OLMS	Office of Labor-Management Standards
OMB	Office of Management and Budget
OPIC	Overseas Private Investment Corporation
OSHA	Occupational Safety and Health Administration
PMA	power marketing administration
PRIVCORP	private corporation
R&D	research and development
SEAB	Secretary of Energy Advisory Board
SEC	U.S. Securities and Exchange Commission
TVA	Tennessee Valley Authority
USEC	U.S. Enrichment Corporation
USPS	U.S. Postal Service
WIPP	Waste Isolation Pilot Plant

CHAPTER ONE

Introduction

Finding ways to safely store and ultimately dispose of used fuel from commercial and defense reactors as well as high-level nuclear waste from defense and other operations has been on the national policy agenda for decades and remains a matter of considerable debate. A new phase of policy review commenced when President Barack Obama announced his decision in January 2010 to withdraw the U.S. Department of Energy's (DOE's) license application for a repository at Yucca Mountain in Nevada, which had been pending before the Nuclear Regulatory Commission (NRC). At the request of the President, the Secretary of Energy subsequently convened a Blue Ribbon Commission on America's Nuclear Future (BRC) "to conduct a comprehensive review of policies for managing the back end of the nuclear fuel cycle" and recommend a new strategy.[1]

Key Findings of the Blue Ribbon Commission

In its February 2012 report on "America's nuclear future," the BRC detailed the history of the nation's efforts to manage, store, and dispose of used fuel and defense high-level nuclear waste, described the complexity of the different tasks that are needed, and outlined a comprehensive strategy to move forward.[2]

Starting with the serious problems confronted in gaining state, tribal, community, and even federal agency support for management and disposition facilities, the BRC recommended a "new consent-based approach" to siting. Further, the BRC noted how a dedicated funding source for nuclear waste management established in the 1982 Nuclear Waste Policy Act (NWPA) became instead a discretionary and unstable funding source through various budgetary acts on the part of Congress and previous administrations. This finding led to another key BRC recommendation that, for any future efforts to be successful, it was imperative that those responsible for managing

---

[1]   DOE, 2010a.

[2]   BRC, 2012.

nuclear waste have access to the Nuclear Waste Fund (NWF), whose revenues are raised from nuclear utility ratepayers.

In the past, the DOE Office of Civilian Radioactive Waste Management (OCRWM) had responsibility for the management and disposition of used fuel and defense high-level nuclear waste. Stakeholders and many other observers noted problems with that assignment of responsibility. In response, the BRC called for a new organization outside of DOE dedicated solely to developing and implementing a program for siting, transportation, storage, and disposition of used fuel and defense high-level nuclear waste.

The BRC found that OCRWM had been given both too little attention because it had to compete for resources within a multi-mission cabinet-level department (DOE) and too much attention because it was subject to a broad range of public oversight and accountability measures, including annual congressional appropriations. The BRC noted that OCRWM was headed by a director who was a presidential appointee, which led to turnover of senior managers with every new administration and, at times, even more frequently. Because OCRWM was inside the federal government, it was bound by civil service personnel rules, under pressure to meet deadlines without control of its funding, and confronted by an inherent lack of flexibility to respond to changing conditions and to negotiate agreements with state and community stakeholders.

The Concept: A Federal Corporation for Waste Management

Given these problems, the BRC called for "a new organization dedicated solely to implementing the waste management program and empowered with the authority and resources to succeed."[3] While emphasizing the need for outstanding, inspired leadership and admitting that multiple possibilities exist for what this new organization could be, the BRC recommended "as the most promising model" the creation of an organization chartered by Congress and structured as a federal government corporation.[4]

Through legislation, Congress would define the new organization's mission and responsibilities, its governance structure, its regulatory and legal environment, and its accountability, both to the American public at large and its stakeholders in affected states, tribal lands, and communities and to the utilities operating nuclear plants. The BRC further envisioned that the new organization would have its own dedicated funding source (to cover the portion of its responsibilities associated with storage and disposition of commercial used fuel) and hence be exempt from federal government

---

[3] BRC, 2012, p. vii.

[4] BRC, 2012, p. x.

budgetary regulations and congressional appropriations.[5] Congressional and executive branch oversight would be achieved through annual policy and financial management reporting.

The BRC suggested that the new organization would be held accountable through a board of directors drawn from various stakeholders nominated by the President and confirmed by the Senate. The board would have responsibility for setting the organization's strategic direction and for reviewing its performance against targets and goals. The board would appoint the chief executive officer (CEO), who would serve set but renewable terms. The organization would operate its own personnel, procurement, and administrative support systems, as well as own and operate the facilities needed to manage the disposal of nuclear waste. Its funds would come from the existing NWF, and if government-owned materials were also within its responsibilities, from the federal government.[6]

The new organization would have a legal personality distinct from the U.S. government, so it could enter into contracts and be sued, making private contracts more enforceable. It would be subject to the same federal and state health, safety, and environmental regulations as any public or private entity, including from the NRC and the Environmental Protection Agency (EPA).

The idea of creating a government corporation to manage used nuclear materials is not new. In 1984, the Advisory Panel on Alternative Means of Financing and Managing Radioactive Waste Facilities (known as AMFM) analyzed ten organizational alternatives and recommended the creation of a federal corporation for waste management (FEDCORP).[7] In its response to this proposal, DOE argued at the time against organizational change "during the critical siting and licensing phase of the program" and raised concerns that such an organization would be more difficult than DOE to be held accountable politically.[8] In 2001, DOE again studied an "independent federal authority" as one of three longer-term management alternatives, recommending continued analysis and refinement of the concept.[9] More recently, after describing how the United States and other countries have managed defense high-level nuclear waste, the U.S. Nuclear Waste Technical Review Board (NWTRB) concluded that no organizational form emerged as superior among the international examples studied; in particular, the board noted that both nuclear industry–owned corporations (Sweden and

---

[5]   Funding to cover expenses related to management, storage, transportation, and disposition of defense high-level nuclear waste and other waste now under DOE's control would continue to be funded through appropriations.

[6]   The BRC noted that revisiting the complex question of whether national policy should continue to allow the commingling of commercial and government-owned waste was beyond its mandate but worthy of further study.

[7]   AMFM, 1984. An extensive critique of the AMFM report can be found in Craig Thomas, "AF-FM Corporate Solutions for Radioactive Waste Management: Appealing But Inappropriate?" in SEAB, 1993, pp. 307–366.

[8]   Review Group, 1985.

[9]   DOE, 2001.

Finland) and a government agency (France) appear to be successful thus far in their operations.[10]

Study Objectives and Approach

DOE asked RAND to support its effort to respond to the recommendations of the BRC and to focus on what organization should be created to manage and dispose of used fuel and defense high-level nuclear waste—hereafter referred to as a management and disposition organization (MDO).

As noted above, the BRC concluded that a congressionally chartered federal government corporation offers particular advantages to solving the problem of managing and disposing of used fuel and defense high-level nuclear waste, but it also acknowledged that "previous studies have concluded that a number of different organizational forms could also get the job done."[11] Thus, this study takes as its point of departure the need for a new organization (an MDO) and goes on to systematically analyze different organizational models. Most organizational studies are quite out of date; they also do not take into account the recent history of unsuccessful efforts to site or construct either centralized storage or a permanent repository site.

Our research approach combined reviews of the considerable literature on organizing to carry out used fuel and defense high-level nuclear waste management, including the reports and background papers of the BRC and interviews with people who have been involved in nuclear waste management in the past, as well as those who have experiences in managing government and private corporations and government agencies.

We begin in Chapter Two by taking a retrospective look to ask what the major problems were in nuclear waste management in past decades and where responsibility for those problems lies: with enabling legislation, with implementing actions by Congress and the executive branch and state and local governments, or with other factors?

In Chapter Three, we then explore potential organizational models, paying specific attention to federal government corporations (GOVCORPs) but also to federally chartered private corporations (PRIVCORPs) and independent government agencies (IGAs). We describe their characteristics and how they perform their specific missions. We look at real-world examples of each type of organizational model. Even though the missions of most of these organizations are very different from management and disposition of used fuel and defense high-level nuclear waste, the real-world examples provided us with the means to define a set of generic organizational models that we then describe in terms of their structure of governance, their accountability to Congress and

---

[10] NWTRB, 2011, p. xvii.

[11] BRC, 2012, p. 61.

the executive branch of government, and their relationships with other stakeholders, such as states, tribes, local communities, the nuclear industry, and affected publics.

Although choices could be made among these theoretical models based solely on their characteristics, we discovered that more analysis was required, with a focus on the critical attributes an organization would needs to achieve its performance goals and carry out its responsibilities. So, in Chapter Four, we describe the complex and unique responsibilities of the new MDO, its performance goals, the critical organizational attributes, and the structural and procedural features that support achievement of the attributes and, by extension, the goals. We then assess whether these features exist or could be built into one or more of the organizational models.

In Chapter Five we conclude with a description of the choices facing policymakers in the design of a new MDO: first about the relationship of the MDO to the President, next about Congress's role, third about the source of the MDO's funding, and then the role of stakeholders and other MDO organizational features.

This document also contains three appendixes. Appendix A describes two real-world examples of organizations that blend the features of private corporations and government agencies: the Tennessee Valley Authority (TVA) and Bonneville Power Administration (BPA). Appendix B provides a tabular summary of the major characteristics of Swedish and Canadian MDOs, as examples of foreign, nongovernment models. Appendix C, which excerpts the statute codifying the Government Corporation Control Act (GCCA) (specifically, 31 U.S.C. § 9101), lists some of the mixed-ownership government corporations and the wholly owned government corporations.

CHAPTER TWO

Learning Lessons from the Past

This chapter sets the stage for analyzing possible organizational models for the new MDO. It looks back and asks what the major problems in nuclear waste management were in past decades and where responsibility lies for those problems. Specifically, were the problems with the enabling legislation; the implementing actions by Congress, the White House, DOE (including OCRWM); the regulating agencies (NRC and EPA); state and local governments; or others, including stakeholders and the general public? Applying lessons and experience from the past will help policymakers design a new MDO.

Assessment of the Prior Organizational Design

Critiques of the federal government's execution of the NWPA are abundant, including from the U.S. Government Accountability Office (GAO) and DOE's inspector general (IG).[1] Most recently, the BRC critique integrated the findings of many of these previous studies with new testimonials and concluded that past actions by the federal government had the cumulative effect of eroding the public trust to the point at which any effort to rebuild trust within the rubric of the current organizational design of an office within DOE was unlikely to succeed.[2] A corollary to this proposition is that a new organization laboring under the same conditions that contributed to past problems is unlikely to meet with more success than a new and improved OCRWM.

In undertaking our brief review of the sources of past problems here, our intent is not to assign blame; instead, we are looking to identify linkages, if any, between

---

[1]   GAO has published more than 100 reports since 1982 about OCRWM and, subsequent to the 1987 Nuclear Waste Policy Act Amendments (Pub. L. 100-202, Pub. L. 100-203), its execution of the Yucca Mountain program. For a recent summary, see GAO, 2011. For a full listing, search the GAO website for the phrase "Nuclear Waste Policy Act" and the word "implementation." Similarly, the DOE IG has published many reports on OCRWM as well. See, for example, DOE, 2006. For a full listing, search DOE, undated, for "OCRWM." Also see SEAB, 1993; Easterling and Kunreuther, 1995; and Macfarlane and Ewing, 2006.

[2]   BRC, 2012, pp. 23–24.

organizational structure and performance that emerged since the time of passage of the 1982 NWPA.

Our analysis of such past problems drew on publicly available documents and the views and insights of experts with experience managing nuclear waste both inside and outside the government. It focuses on these five areas:

- governance and leadership
- funding and budget control
- siting process
- procurement and personnel rules
- public trust.

Governance and Leadership

Section 304 of the NWPA established OCRWM within DOE and made the director of OCRWM a Senate-confirmed presidential appointee who reported directly to the Secretary of Energy. Views differ about whether OCRWM's placement in DOE was, in and of itself, a major contributor to the failure of the program to meet deadlines and gain public trust.[3] The critique has two aspects: lack of priority for OCRWM within DOE and leadership turnover within OCRWM linked to turnover of the leadership in DOE.

As the BRC expressed, placing OCRWM within a large cabinet agency made it difficult for DOE to concentrate on the NWPA's objectives "when balancing multiple agency agendas and policy priorities."[4] This is not the same as saying that the program lacked sustained or sufficient attention from DOE secretaries because they were too busy doing other things, although some have suggested that that was the case.[5] Rather, DOE secretaries, as is true for all secretaries in cabinet-level agencies, face a zero-sum game with respect to programs within their department. OCRWM, along with all the other programs within DOE, had to compete for its share of the annual budget that the Office of Management and Budget (OMB) allotted to DOE and then meet the same challenge within the annual congressional appropriations process.[6]

The short-term nature of the annual agency budgeting process ensured that neither the secretary nor Congress would squarely face the implications of chronic underfunding of the OCRWM program, eventually leading to the breach of contracts from

---

[3] It should be noted that, delays notwithstanding, the program did, in fact, succeed in developing a license application for the Yucca Mountain site.

[4] BRC, 2012, p. 61.

[5] In the early years of the program, former DOE officials and industry representatives noted that OCRWM was not always a high priority within DOE and that the quality of managers running the program varied, attributing these conditions to a lack of commitment to the program (GAO, 2011).

[6] BRC, 2012, p. 24.

the missed 1998 deadline to take title to the used fuel generated by the utilities (discussed more next in the "Funding and Budget Control" section). As far back as 1993, GAO noted,

> DOE has been requesting far lower appropriations for characterizing Yucca Mountain than the agency had determined were needed to complete the task on schedule. This disparity is due to competition among all of the agency's programs for funds as well as competing priorities within the disposal program.[7]

The BRC also noted that DOE and OCRWM experienced frequent turnover in leadership. With few exceptions, cabinet officers change when administrations change. However, in DOE's case, secretaries often changed more frequently (ten secretaries serving five presidents between 1982 and the present). OCRWM directors often changed when secretaries changed.[8] Lack of continuity in leadership led to a lack of continuity in policy and priorities, further contributing to the lurches in the program's direction and progress toward licensing a repository at Yucca Mountain and ultimately taking title to the used commercial fuel.[9] Lack of continuity in leadership further undermined OCRWM and DOE's accountability to Congress and the public.

Presidents have control over the tenures of cabinet officers within the limits of their terms. Presidents and cabinet officers can also agree on informal tenure limits for key positions with the express purpose of achieving continuity, durability, and some insulation from political forces. An example of this is the long-standing executive branch tradition of having the term of the director of the U.S. Geological Survey extend beyond changes in administration. Congress also can specify terms of key leadership positions, as it does with the ten-year term of the director of the Federal Bureau of Investigation or the staggered 14-year terms of the governors of the Federal Reserve Bank. Neither of these mechanisms was adopted in the case of the directorship of OCRWM.

In summary, the enabling legislation establishing OCRWM within DOE is at the core of the problems associated with the lack of continuity in leadership. The executive branch also shares responsibility for not moving toward a more stable and durable leadership structure within its available powers. DOE's difficulties in securing adequate and sustained funding arose from other sources and are discussed below.

Funding and Budget Control

Section 302 of the NWPA established the NWF. The clear intent of the legislation was to provide a stable source of funding under the control of the Secretary of Energy for repository development, construction, and related operations. The statutory language

---

[7]   GAO, 1993.

[8]   BRC, 2012, p. 61.

[9]   GAO, 2011.

makes clear that the NWF was to be the implementing mechanism for the "user pays" principle: Ratepayers benefiting from nuclear power would pay one mill ($0.001 per kilowatt-hour) to cover the estimated costs of disposition of the used fuel as envisioned in the act. The quid pro quo memorialized in contracts with each of the utilities was that OCRWM would secure an NRC license to open a repository by 1998. At that time, DOE would take title to the used fuel from the utilities and begin the process of transport, short-term storage, and, ultimately, emplacement at the repository site.

However, congressional attempts to rein in government spending essentially nullified the user-pays principle of the NWF. The Gramm-Rudman-Hollings Balanced Budget and Emergency Deficit Control Act of 1985, followed by the Budget Enforcement Act of 1990, changed the rules.[10] As a way for Congress to gain greater control of government spending, nearly all discretionary spending (including special funds, such as the NWF) controlled through the annual appropriations process was also placed under statutory caps. The total spending caps, combined with the appropriations requirement in the 1982 NWPA, severely limited the ability of the secretary to prescribe the level of spending for the OCRWM program. As the BRC noted,

> [t]he Fund does not work as intended. A series of executive branch and congressional actions has made annual fee revenues (approximately $750 million per year) and the unspent $27 billion balance in the Fund effectively inaccessible to the waste program. Instead, the waste program must compete for federal funding each year and is therefore subject to exactly the budget constraints and uncertainties that the Fund was created to avoid.[11]

Without adjusting either the scope of the program or the timelines under which the program was operating, OCRWM experienced budget shortfalls every year relative to what the program required and the secretary requested. Often, both OMB and Congress substantially reduced DOE's requested budget for the program.[12] Unsurprisingly, the program fell behind, and milestones were routinely missed. There were insufficient funds for all the activities needed to run in parallel to keep the program on track to meet the 1998 deadline. Priority went to keeping the licensing process moving forward, but activities related to transportation, for example, were virtually zeroed out. OCRWM followed a strategy of maintaining a baseline level of activities to enable it to ramp up if more funding materialized; it never did.

---

[10]   Pub. L. 99-177 and Pub. L. 101-508, respectively. The Gramm-Rudman-Hollings Act to control deficit spending was first passed in 1985 and then revised in 1987 after the Supreme Court found the mandatory cuts required by the earlier version unconstitutional (*Bowsher v Synar*, 478 U.S. 714, 1986).

[11]   BRC, 2012, p. xi. See also U.S. Department of Energy, Office of Civilian Radioactive Waste Management, *Alternative Means of Financing and Managing the Civilian Radioactive Waste Management Program*, 2001.

[12]   OCRWM's annual appropriations varied by as much as 20 percent from year to year, and its average annual shortfall of appropriations from its budget request was about $90 million each year (GAO, 2011).

Regardless of leadership in the White House or Congress, OCRWM's budget stayed well below the budget DOE determined was required to meet the deadlines in the NWPA. This was an enduring problem for OCRWM. For most federal programs, reduced appropriations simply mean stretched timelines. However, for a program such as OCRWM, that had a hard deadline after which major liabilities arise from breach of contractual obligations, the underfunding of the program had large future consequences for federal spending.[13] Within the annual budget and appropriations processes, there was no incentive to spend money in the near term to keep the program on track even though it would have led to saving money in the long term by avoiding liability payments to the utilities. Hence, the 1998 deadline passed with no prospect in sight of the federal government taking title to the commercial used fuel.

In sum, as a program within DOE, OCRWM became a victim of the changes made in the budget and appropriations processes that limited the secretary's access to the NWF. Although OCRWM's organizational position within DOE was a contributing factor in its funding shortfall, the budget and accounting decisions to make OCRWM spending subject to the annual appropriations cycle with no credit for receipts had an even greater impact.

Siting Process

Title I of the NWPA prescribed the siting process for repositories for used fuel and defense high-level nuclear waste and for a "monitored retrievable storage" facility, or MRS. In the 1982 NWPA, Congress envisioned that several candidate sites would be characterized through detailed scientific and engineering studies and two sites would be selected, with the implication that one would end up in the east and the other one in the west. Consent of states and tribes was desired but not required; no specific mention was made of communities. The NWPA laid out a mechanism in which Congress could override a governor's objection to siting a repository within his or her state through a simple majority in each house of Congress.

In the 1987 amendments to the NWPA, Congress short-circuited its previously authorized siting process and instead decided that site characterization would proceed only at the Yucca Mountain site in Nevada, with no further work on siting a second repository. Congress took this action over the objections of the State of Nevada. Texas and Washington, with sites under study, had also registered strong objections. Further, the cost of carrying forward detailed site characterization studies at multiple locations of varying geology was significant. In short, under the terms and conditions for siting on the table in the 1980s, no state with a site under study at the time wanted a repository within its borders.

Belatedly, in the 1987 amendments, Congress created a position of the nuclear waste negotiator, reporting directly to the President, with an office to support the nego-

---

[13] Clearly, the absence of consent from Nevada, noted in the next section, was another major contributor.

tiator's activities to secure a repository site. Congress even spelled out a benefit package with the express purpose of helping to move along the siting of the MRS. However, the position was not filled until 1990. By then, Congress had decided against the siting of an MRS, despite multiple volunteer sites. The Office of the Nuclear Waste Negotiator was closed in 1995.[14]

The bottom line was that there was no "winning play" on siting, as one observer noted, no ability to achieve consensus under the terms of the NWPA, and indeed no way Nevada would come around to accepting the Yucca Mountain site in the absence of a tectonic shift in the state's leadership and the federal government's orientation to siting. As the BRC and other close observers have noted, the decisions by Congress to proceed with Yucca Mountain over Nevada's objections had the effect of undermining the legitimacy of the program, eroding public trust, and ultimately leading to the demise of the program.[15] Not only was the public trust eroded. DOE's missed deadlines, breach of contract, and finally, the President's decision to withdraw the Yucca Mountain license application attracted criticism from the nuclear industry and utilities.[16]

In sum, the failure to site and license a repository or MRS facility and the failure to proceed with an NRC-licensed private storage facility in Utah reflect a breakdown in national policy implementation.[17] Yet, given the statutory, regulatory, and budgetary framework within which OCRWM was compelled to operate, it is difficult to associate these siting failures with organizational design per se. Rather, the 1982 NWPA, in which a state's consent was not a requirement, and the subsequent 1987 amendments to the NWPA set the terms and conditions that ultimately determined the fate of these several siting processes.

Federal Procurement and Personnel Policies

When we asked former senior managers of OCRWM and DOE about factors contributing to OCRWM's difficulties in performing at a high level, they cited funding constraints as the single most important factor. But just as often, they cited the constraints of operating under federal procurement and personnel rules as the next contributing factor. These officials cited procurement of technical, management, and consulting services as an example of OCRWM's difficulty in operating in an efficient manner. With

---

[14] "Nuclear Waste Negotiator Office," undated.

[15] See, e.g., BRC, 2012, p. 23. See also SEAB, 1993, and Easterling and Kunreuther, 1995.

[16] See Marvin S. Fertel, President and Chief Executive Officer, Nuclear Energy Institute, Testimony before the U.S. House of Representatives Appropriations Subcommittee on Energy and Water Development, Washington, D.C., March 19, 2010.

[17] BRC, 2012, p. 24; *Devia v NRC*, 492 F. 3d 421 (D.C. Cir., June 26, 2007). Private Fuel Services, an industry consortium, sought and received a license from the NRC to operate a storage facility on the Skull Valley Goshute Reservation, but the Bureau of Land Management and the Bureau of Indian Affairs, both within the U.S. Department of the Interior, blocked approval of a lease and rights of way.

no special provisions to the contrary in the NWPA, OCRWM, like any other federal agency, was bound by the Federal Acquisition Regulation System (the FARS). This complex body of administrative procedures prescribes how agencies procure a wide range of services and goods. As it related to OCRWM, the FARS largely dictated the way in which the program procured a contractor, known as the management and operations (M&O) contractor, through a competitive bidding process. According to GAO, OCRWM did not get the M&O contractor it wanted at a critical time in 1989 because of legal challenges to the initial selection.[18] Congress could have provided explicit relief from the Federal Acquisition Regulation (FAR) but did not do so. Whether outcomes of the OCRWM program indeed would have been different under alternatives to standard federal procurement rules cannot be known. While differences between government and commercial procurement processes can be significant, particularly in terms of efficiency, there is no basis for concluding that operating under a different set of rules would have fundamentally changed OCRWM's performance. Commercial procurement has its difficulties as well.[19]

Former officials also note constraints that working within the federal personnel system imposed on their ability to carry out their mission. One official flatly stated that NRC-level performance standards "cannot be met under the Federal personnel system."[20] The problem had less to do with attracting top talent to the program than with changing out poor performers, which was and remains very difficult. Over time, former officials noted, OCRWM got weighed down with underperforming staff in key senior positions. As with procurement rules, it is difficult to know how these constraints may have affected performance.

In sum, Congress could have exempted OCRWM, in whole or in part, from federal procurement and personnel rules but chose not to do so. A congressional exemption from standard administrative procedures is indeed a rare, albeit not impossible, hurdle to overcome for an ordinary government agency. There are good reasons why most of these rules are in place including the need for public accountability and transparency, hence the reluctance of Congress to provide exemptions.

Public Trust

With the possible exception of real or perceived difficulties with the procurement and personnel rules, each of the problems described in this section contributed to the erosion of public trust in OCRWM, DOE, Congress, and indeed the siting process itself.

---

[18] GAO, 1989.

[19] Cavinato and Kauffman, 2000, pp. 1029–1069; Merrow, 2011, Chapter 11. There are a number of important differences between government and commercial procurement, particularly in the balance struck among transparency, fairness, aversion to risk of any kind, and efficiency. Much of this literature is also cited in an excellent compendium of the social science literature found in SEAB, 1993.

[20] Personal communication to the authors, April 13, 2012.

As the BRC noted, Congress's selection of Yucca Mountain and the elimination of other sites for consideration set the program at odds with a basic sense of fairness, due process, and accountability.[21]

The erosion of trust in public institutions is not particular to management and disposition of nuclear waste, but it was perhaps magnified in this instance by the history of secrecy and missteps in DOE that preceded the establishment of OCRWM in the 1982 NWPA. Further, an extensive social science literature dating back more than 30 years documents the fundamentally different way in which many members of the public perceive the risks of nuclear power and radioactivity.[22] In effect, OCRWM began its life under the handicap of low levels of public trust engendered by DOE and its predecessor agencies, and it never managed to rise above its legacy.

Another factor contributing to the loss of public trust was related to regulations promulgated by the NRC and EPA. As part of the 1987 amendments, Congress required the NRC to develop "site-specific" regulations for Yucca Mountain, leaving the impression, as the BRC noted, of stacking the deck in favor of approval of the site. Further, in 1995, Congress ordered the National Research Council of the National Academy of Sciences to review EPA's human health and environmental radiation protection standards that a Yucca Mountain repository would need to meet. The National Research Council study committee came back with a recommendation, among others, that the repository should be shown capable of meeting an individual protection standard 1 million years from now.[23] These changes in regulation, perhaps justified in isolation, contributed to an impression of changing rules in the middle of the game, not only for Nevada but also for other stakeholders and OCRWM itself.

Organizations earn the public's trust through their demonstration of accountability, transparency, technical credibility, and bottom-line performance.[24] Trust cannot be ensured through any particular organizational form, public or private. Indeed, the kind of organizational performance that engenders trust does not necessarily follow from organizational form, as is well documented in the literature.[25] It is difficult to overstate the role that Congress played in undermining the public's trust in DOE and OCRWM through the 1987 amendments to the NWPA. At the same time, DOE and OCRWM fell short in their communications with the public, particularly the Nevada public. As the NWTRB discovered in the late 1990s, its public meetings held in various locations in Nevada several times per year became the venue for citizens to ask questions directly to DOE management and staff who were, or appeared to be, other-

---

[21] BRC, 2012, p. 23.

[22] Fischhoff et al., 1978; Fischhoff, 1983; see also Slovic, Fischhoff, and Lichtenstein, 1982.

[23] EPA, 2011.

[24] La Porte and Metlay, 1996.

[25] See Craig Thomas, "Reorganizing Public Organizations: Alternatives, Objectives, and Evidence," in SEAB, 1993, pp. 261–305.

wise inaccessible. By then, DOE placed its efforts on working through its milestones on the path to a license application. The actions of the regulators, complying with statutory and other congressional instructions, did little to overcome the lack of trust that already clouded the program.

Conclusions

The organizational design of OCRWM within DOE contributed less to the problems encountered in implementation than the NWPA itself and subsequent congressional and executive branch actions. These actions included most notably the 1987 amendments when Yucca Mountain was selected as the only candidate repository site over the objections of Nevada, and then several years later, changes in budgeting that severely constrained the Secretary's access to the NWF. In the light of OCRWM's history and the actions of Congress and various administrations as a whole, perhaps the most important lesson to be drawn is that organizational form may only have a limited effect on a program's performance; it is a necessary but not sufficient condition for success. As flawed as OCRWM's program implementation may have been at times, it is difficult to imagine that any organization could have successfully executed the program in the absence of both public support in the affected state and sustained funding from Congress, itself an indicator of public support.

For these reasons, the BRC focused its findings and recommendations on the need to change the funding arrangements and commit to a consent-based siting approach as preconditions for laying the groundwork for gaining public trust and support. The focus of this study is to support choices about the characteristics, critical attributes, and features of an organization that could at once cultivate and reinforce the values that will lead to success. In the next chapter, we compare and contrast the characteristics of various organizational forms.

CHAPTER THREE

Exploring Potential Organizational Models

Presidents and Congress have historically turned to GOVCORPs when looking for ways to combine some of the features of private corporations with those of government agencies. But there are other ways to accomplish this blending. One way is to create a private corporation that is federally chartered (PRIVCORP), while another is to create an independent government agency (IGA).[1] Broadly speaking, these three models can be understood as falling on a continuum that ranges from purely private-sector organizations at one extreme, to traditional government agencies at the other (see Figure 3.1).

In this chapter, we develop and characterize these three organizational models that could each constitute a new single-purpose, nuclear material MDO. We begin with the GOVCORP, the organization recommended by the BRC. Within our analysis of the three models, we seek to illuminate their key, prototypical characteristics:

- congressional charter
- direct oversight and roles of President and Congress
- funding, financial management oversight, and borrowing authority

Figure 3.1
The Organizational Spectrum: Private to Public Sector

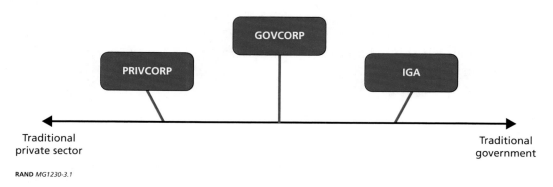

RAND *MG1230-3.1*

---

[1]   The key distinction here is between an ordinary private corporation (chartered under state law) and a private corporation that is federally chartered (by Congress). The latter is a PRIVCORP by our definition, while the former is not.

- role of stakeholders[2]
- ownership of entity
- regulatory obligations
- legal liabilities
- personnel management, procurement, and contracting.

In addition to the prototypical characteristics of the three models, we also identify major aspects of variation within each organizational model. These variations could be useful as background to policymakers designing an MDO because they could be as crucial to the success of an MDO as the organizational form itself. Finally, we identify major points of similarity and difference between the organizational models, which may offer reasons for preferring one model to another in the design for an MDO. Appendix A contains a more detailed comparison that highlights two real-world examples: TVA, a GOVCORP, and BPA, an IGA reporting to the Secretary of Energy.

Note that countries other than the United States have created organizations with a range of different governance structures to manage nuclear material, with varying degrees of success. At one end of the spectrum lie Belgium, Germany, the Republic of Korea, and the United Kingdom, which are purely public, government agencies. At the other end of the spectrum are Canada, Finland, Japan, and Sweden, which use primarily non-governmental, for-profit or non-profit models. Between these two extremes, China, France, Spain, and Switzerland use government-owned corporations or public-private partnerships. We reviewed several of these non-U.S. organizational examples in compiling this report. For illustration, Appendix B provides a tabular summary of the major characteristics of Swedish and Canadian MDOs, as examples of foreign, nongovernment models.[3]

In sum, we find that the models involve different avenues for blending the features of a private-sector organization (e.g., independence and flexibility) and of a government agency (e.g., public trust, congressional and executive branch influence). The key takeaway of this examination lies in the flexibility the U.S. government has in establishing different kinds of organizations to carry out unique missions and to solve particular problems. Policymakers face choices not only among the different organizational models but also in how they design the structure of a particular organization once its form is chosen.

---

[2]   When we discuss the "role of stakeholders" and "stakeholder engagement" in this chapter, we are uniformly referring to stakeholders in the broadest possible sense: i.e., anyone with a legitimate interest in the public consequences of organizational decisionmaking. Stakeholders in the MDO context could plausibly include a wide range of different interest groups, as we discuss elsewhere in this report.

[3]   For in-depth discussions of national nuclear waste organizations, see International Atomic Energy Agency (IAEA), 2007; NWTRB, 2009, 2011.

Comparison of Organizational Models

This chapter begins with a description of the federal government corporation, or GOV-CORP, as it is the recommendation of the BRC, and the chapter then goes on to compare GOVCORP characteristics with those of a federally chartered private corporation (PRIVCORP) and an independent government agency (IGA). See Table 3.1 for a summary of the characteristics of the three models.

Federal Government Corporation

The GOVCORP is a hybrid form of organization involving a government instrumentality that combines some of the characteristics of a private-sector corporation with those of a traditional government agency. Notably, the GOVCORP organizational model does not appear to have a widely accepted, formal definition. Typically, public administration scholars and officials endorse President Harry S. Truman's description of GOVCORP characteristics, which stated that

> the corporate form of organization is peculiarly adapted to the administration of governmental programs which are *predominantly of a commercial character*—those which are *revenue producing*, are at least *potentially self-sustaining*, and *involve a large number of business-type transactions with the public*. In their business operations such programs *require greater flexibility* than the customary type of appropriation budget ordinarily permits. (emphasis added)[4]

However, these defining features of the GOVCORP have never been formally codified into law, and the resulting ambiguity has sometimes led scholars to different conclusions about what constitutes a GOVCORP and about how many GOVCORPs there actually are. Although Chapter 91 of Title 31 of the U.S. Code, also known as the GCCA,[5] provides a list of entities that it defines as "government corporations," that list is illustrative rather than exhaustive, and several unlisted entities have also notably been subject to GCCA provisions.[6] Today, the GCCA formally lists 11 mixed-ownership government corporations and 17 wholly owned government corporations. See Appendix C for this list.

Here, we define a GOVCORP as a federally chartered government instrumentality, typically formed with a commercial purpose, that is subject to some level of federal

---

[4]   Truman, 1947.

[5]   31 U.S.C. 9101 et seq. The GCCA establishes standards for GOVCORP budgeting, auditing, and reporting, although Congress obviously retains the option to exempt new GOVCORPs from any of those requirements via charter.

[6]   In 2009, GAO identified four federally created entities not listed in the GCCA yet subject to its provisions (GAO, 2009).

Table 3.1
Comparison of Organizational Models

Characteristics	PRIVCORP	GOVCORP	IGA
Charter	Act of Congress defines mission and structure	Act of Congress defines mission and structure	Act of Congress defines mission and structure
Direct oversight	Board of directors (on behalf of stockholders)	Board of directors (on behalf of executive branch of government)	Administrator, commission, or executive board
Role of President and White House	Nothing formal	President nominates board of directors OMB reviews annual management and financial reports	President nominates administrator or members of executive board or commission OMB may exercise oversight and approve annual budgets
Role of Congress	No regular oversight	Senate may confirm members of board of directors House and Senate committee review of strategic plans and annual management and financial reports Some GAO oversight	Senate may confirm administrator or members of executive board or commission House and Senate committees review annual reports on operations and approve annual budgets GAO oversight
Funding	For profit	Not for profit or for profit (depending on whether wholly owned by government); mostly commercial enterprises pay expenditures from operating revenues ("self-sustaining"); some receive congressional appropriation	Most receive annual congressional appropriation, but can be set up to pay expenditures from operating revenues ("self-sustaining")
Role of stakeholders	Stockholder meetings; stockholders directly represented by board of directors	Advisory boards and committees; possible representation for diverse stakeholder groups on board of directors	Advisory boards and committees; possible representation for diverse stakeholder groups on executive board or commission
Borrowing authority	Sell bonds to public; not backed by U.S. government	Sell bonds to public and to Treasury, depending on the terms of federal charter or executive order	From Treasury, backed by the full faith and credit of the federal government
Ownership of entity	Private stockholders	U.S. government and sometimes private stockholders	U.S. government

Table 3.1—Continued

Characteristics	PRIVCORP	GOVCORP	IGA
Regulatory obligations	Same as for private-sector entities generally, unless specifically exempted by Congress in charter	Not subject to some regulatory requirements that apply only to private-sector corporations (e.g., some forms of federal securities regulation); Congress can waive other types of regulation via charter	Subject to federal regulations; not subject to some regulatory requirements that apply only to private-sector corporations
Legal liabilities	Generally subject to private civil claims	Generally subject to private civil claims, but possibly with some sovereign protection for employees	Has sovereign immunity and Federal Tort Claims Act (FTCA) limits on vulnerability to civil claims
Personnel management, procurement, contracting	Private sector; not subject to government administrative rules since PRIVCORPs by definition are not government entities	Tend to be subject to more federal administrative requirements than PRIVCORPs but less than IGAs	Typically subject to federal administrative requirements

NOTE: The entries in the table represent the prototypical characteristics of each of the organizational models. However, Congress may, through the legislative charter, mandate different characteristics and has done so in the past.

government control and ownership but that also follows some aspects of the corporate form, including (in most instances) primary oversight by a board of directors.[7]

Congressional Charter

The process for forming a GOVCORP involves the legislative action of Congress and the enactment of a formal federal charter specifying the purpose, powers, structure, and obligations of the new entity.[8] Unlike private corporations, which are formed subject to the general corporation laws of a specific state, GOVCORPs are formed under federal authority. Thus, Congress has considerably more latitude in defining the parameters for a new GOVCORP than is the case for the creators of a new private corporation formed under state law. Although some broad legal contours for GOVCORPs are laid out under the GCCA, the main authority that determines the structure and purpose of any individual GOVCORP is its own federal charter, as laid down by Congress.[9]

---

[7] Despite the foregoing definition, it is important to note that not all GOVCORPs actually have a board of directors. Ginnie Mae is an example of wholly owned GOVCORP that does not, and instead simply has an administrator appointed by the President. See discussion in Kosar, 2011.

[8] Examples of congressional charters creating GOVCORPs include the Tennessee Valley Authority Act of 1933 (Pub. L. 73-17), the Rail Passenger Service Act of 1970 (creating Amtrak) (Pub. L. 91-518), and the Communications Satellite Act of 1962 (creating the Communications Satellite Corporation [COMSAT]) (Pub. L. 87-26).

[9] Congressional authority to create GOVCORPs derives from the "necessary and proper clause" of the Constitution Article I, § 8, ¶ 18. This clause has served as the foundation for several Supreme Court rulings and case law upholding Congress's ability to create corporations. See *Osborn v President, Directors and Co. of Bank*, 22 U.S. 738

Modification of the charter of a GOVCORP would also require an act of Congress. However, revisions to the structure and function of a GOVCORP consistent with its basic charter provisions (e.g., revisions to its bylaws) can be undertaken without recourse to legislation.

Direct Oversight and the Roles of the President and Congress

Because GOVCORPs tend to mimic some key aspects of a private-sector corporation, most GOVCORPs are subject to oversight by a board of directors.[10] As in a for-profit corporation, the role of the board in a GOVCORP typically involves appointing and monitoring a CEO, as well as performing some level of ongoing fiduciary oversight. The GOVCORP's federal charter determines the structure and size of the GOVCORP's board and the necessary qualifications of its directors.[11] Typically, the power to appoint directors is assigned to the President. Presidential appointment of directors and, in most instances, Senate confirmation of those appointments help to establish that the board is ultimately responsible to the federal government, even though the GOVCORP may otherwise be independent of many of the ordinary channels of executive branch oversight and direction. The right of the President to appoint some or all the members of the governing board means that they (by implication) owe their positions to the President.

Variation in the structure of GOVCORP boards can be seen by looking at TVA (which has a nine-member board, appointed by the President with the advice and consent of the Senate), Amtrak (which has a 15-member board, with eight seats appointed by the President with the advice and consent of the Senate and seven seats determined by stockholder election), and the Communications Satellite Corporation, or COMSAT (which had a 15-member board, with three members appointed by the President and confirmed by the Senate and 12 members elected by the corporation's stockholders).

GOVCORPs as a group tend to be more independent of congressional and executive branch oversight than traditional executive branch agencies or independent government agencies, but less independent than any fully private-sector organization would be. Under the terms of the GCCA, wholly owned GOVCORPs are required to submit annual financial statements to the President (and indirectly to Congress);[12] to regularly

---

(1824); *Federal Land Bank v Bismarck Lumber Co.*, 314 U.S. 95 (1941); and *Pittman v Home Owners' Loan Corp.*, 308 U.S. 21 (1939).

[10] See Kosar, 2011.

[11] The charter also specifies details concerning the term-length of board members, whether the terms of board members will be staggered, etc. Note that Congress has considerable latitude in designing a board structure via the charter to achieve specific governance goals, such as ensuring that board membership is stable over time and that appropriate business and/or technical expertise is represented.

[12] Sections 9103 and 9104 of the GCCA, which concern budget reporting and congressional oversight of budgets for GOVCORPs, do not apply to mixed-ownership GOVCORPs. Sections 9105 and 9106 of the GCCA, however, impose other financial reporting and audit requirements on both mixed-ownership and wholly owned

file audit reports to specified congressional committees; to submit their activities to the investigative and review authority of the Comptroller General of the United States; and to submit an annual management report to Congress and to the executive branch.

Additional congressional oversight may apply in the form of Senate confirmation for members of the board of directors (to the extent specified in a GOVCORP's charter) and, when funded by appropriations, through congressional budgeting and appropriations processes.

Funding, Financial Management Oversight, and Borrowing Authority

According to Kevin Kosar, GOVCORPs are "exempt either individually or collectively from many executive branch budgetary regulations," based on the implicit rationale that they tend to be engaged in commercial activities from which expenditures can be paid for directly out of operating revenues.[13] As noted in the previous section, GOVCORPs do have obligations to report on their budgeting and finances both to the President and to Congress, and Kosar asserts that Congress does have the theoretical authority to intervene and modify a GOVCORP's budget and to "limit the use of [its] corporate funds for any purpose." However, Kosar observes that this authority is very seldom exercised because most of the GOVCORPs do indeed budget their expenditures against their own revenues and, therefore, do not have a direct impact on the larger federal budget or exert any draw against tax revenues.[14] At the same time, some GOVCORPs do receive congressional appropriations. Amtrak is one example, and TVA, through much of its history, another example. In order for a GOVCORP to engage in public debt financing, the power to do so must be specifically conferred by its charter.[15]

Role of Stakeholders

The governing board of a GOVCORP is typically appointed by, and represents, the executive branch of the federal government. In instances in which a GOVCORP has a mixed-ownership model with some private shareholders, the board may also represent the interests of the private shareholders. Note that, in crafting the charter of a GOVCORP, Congress has latitude to establish additional requirements for the qualifications and identity of the board members. So, for example, the board of a GOVCORP can be

---

GOVCORPs alike, Under 31 U.S.C. § 1105(a)(24), the President's budget submission to Congress may include "recommendations on the return of Government capital to the Treasury by a mixed-ownership corporation . . . that the President decides are desirable."

[13] Kosar, 2011.

[14] Congress has, in the past, used the following methods of funding GOVCORPs: direct appropriations of funds, federal borrowing, authorizing user fees or other charges of services to the public, federal ownership of stock, private investment, or financing with actual or implied backing of the federal government (GAO, 2008, p. 15-120).

[15] Examples of GOVCORPs with stipulated borrowing authority include the Pension Benefit Guaranty Corporation (29 U.S.C. § 1305[c]) and the Rural Telephone Bank (7 U.S.C. § 947).

designed to include required seats both for executive branch officials and for private-sector executives (see, e.g., the Overseas Private Investment Corporation [OPIC]). Presumably, Congress could specifically structure the charter of a GOVCORP to require explicit board representation for multiple outside stakeholder groups if it wanted to do so. For example, the TVA board, by charter, must represent the geographic service area, while the OPIC and COMSAT boards have (or had, in COMSAT's case) a mix of government and private-sector members, each representing different stakeholder groups.

In a different vein, a GOVCORP could clearly choose to organize its own subsidiary advisory boards with participation by nongovernment stakeholders, where this is otherwise consistent with the GOVCORP's mission and charter. However, such advisory boards would not have governing control over the actions of the GOVCORP, pursuant to its basic organizational structure. Although there are many other possible avenues by which a GOVCORP might seek to achieve stakeholder engagement, most of these have little to do with the GOVCORP organizational form.

Ownership of Entity

GOVCORPs are, by definition, either partly or wholly owned by the government. The GCCA includes an illustrative list of GOVCORPs that fall into each category (see Appendix C). However, the GCCA does not provide any explanatory definition of either category beyond listing examples.[16] A 1995 GAO report cited the National Academy of Public Administration in observing that *wholly owned GOVCORP* basically refers to an organization that has no private ownership, while *mixed-ownership GOVCORP* does indicate some private ownership interest.[17]

Regulatory Obligations

Because a GOVCORP is neither a traditional for-profit corporation nor a conventional government agency, it is not bound by some of the regulatory requirements that typically apply to either of those types of organizations. A traditional for-profit corporation formed under state law is subject to the business corporation regulatory authority of the state in which it is formed. Moreover, to the extent that that corporation issues equity securities, it may also be subject to U.S. Securities and Exchange Commission (SEC) regulation. Neither of those types of regulation applies to a (wholly owned) GOVCORP. On the government side, Kosar observes that GOVCORPs as a class are not subject to centralized administrative oversight by OMB or any other executive branch agency, although individual GOVCORPs do come under OMB scrutiny "from time to time."[18] Occasionally, Congress may create a separate, independent watchdog

---

[16] For example, per 31 U.S.C. § 9101, wholly owned GOVCORPs include the Overseas Private Investment Corporation (OPIC) and TVA; mixed-ownership GOVCORPs include the Federal Deposit Insurance Corporation and the Resolution Trust Corporation.

[17] GAO, 1995, footnote 6.

[18] Kosar, 2011.

entity with the sole purpose of determining compliance with congressional statutes and regulations by a particular GOVCORP, through the creation of a pertinent Office of Inspector General.[19]

Michael Froomkin suggests that GOVCORPs are frequently exempted from regulation in the form of "civil service rules regarding employee pay and tenure," as well as from requirements under the Freedom of Information Act and (in some cases) the GCCA.[20] However, it is nevertheless entirely possible for a GOVCORP to engage in commercial activities that bring it under the authority of an (unaffiliated) federal regulatory agency, which means that it will become subject to the rules imposed by that agency. TVA, for example, is notably subject to the regulatory authority of FERC (in connection with generating electricity), SEC (in issuing debt securities), and EPA (in connection with the environmental impact of some of its operations).[21] Congress has latitude when writing the charter of a GOVCORP to stipulate any additional kinds of regulation from which that GOVCORP might be especially exempted.

Legal Liabilities

A GOVCORP has unique liability characteristics that are somewhat different from those of a typical government agency. According to Kosar, a wholly owned GOVCORP has fundamentally the same "state character" as a government agency and is typically regarded by the courts as an agency, and its personnel are therefore subject to the same limited waiver of sovereign immunity under the Federal Tort Claims Act (FTCA) as would apply to the personnel of an actual agency. However, Kosar also notes that most GOVCORPs are nevertheless subject to, and may initiate, their own civil claims. Litigation management for many of the GOVCORPs is reportedly decentralized and not handled through the Department of Justice.[22] Froomkin goes further in stating that every GOVCORP "enjoys a separate legal personality . . . and without legislation to the contrary, its investors, including the United States, presumably enjoy limited liability." He then says the United States is not liable for the debts of even a wholly owned GOVCORP, absent a statutory or common-law rule that says otherwise.[23]

---

[19]   Note that Section 9105 of the GCCA specifically contemplates that an IG may be appointed for a GOVCORP, pursuant to the terms of the Inspector General Act of 1978. See 31 U.S.C. § 9105(a).

[20]   Froomkin, 1995.

[21]   See Appendix A for discussion. For another example, note that Amtrak and Conrail, both of which were (at one time) GOVCORPs, still remained subject to pertinent safety regulations promulgated by the Federal Railroad Administration (FRA), other than as exempted by their federal charter provisions.

[22]   Kosar, 2011.

[23]   Froomkin, 1995. At the same time, in a future GOVCORP, depending on how it is structured, it is entirely possible that the terms of the Price-Anderson Act of 1957 (codified 42 USC § 2210) could apply. The Price-Anderson Act involves a set of provisions for insuring the operation of commercial nuclear power plants in the United States, together with a set of related DOE contractor activities, against potentially catastrophic incidents. Without getting deeply into the details, the Price-Anderson Act provides a mechanism to partly insure related

Although the United States may not be technically on the hook to backstop the debt of an insolvent GOVCORP, the government is nevertheless often perceived as an implicit guarantor of GOVCORP debts and liabilities—a fact that can make it easier for a GOVCORP to obtain credit than would otherwise be true of a private entity. Moreover, the fact that GOVCORPs are capable of being sued without their consent has the effect of making it easier and cheaper for them to enter into contracts than is the case for traditional agencies, because resolution of GOVCORP contract disputes does not need to progress through the laborious U.S. Court of Federal Claims process that would otherwise apply.

Personnel Management, Procurement, and Contracting Mechanisms

GOVCORPs are sometimes independent of some of the administrative obligations that ordinarily apply to government agencies (e.g., in procurement, contracting, personnel management, and budgeting), although likewise unable to take advantage of some of the benefits that accrue to government agencies (most notably, broad assumption of immunity from private civil tort claims). Kosar notably describes GOVCORPs as being subject to "little central management agency oversight or supervision" and as "discrete entities, each with its own administrative requirements, and each with its own route and degree of political accountability."[24]

Under the Office of Federal Procurement Policy Act,[25] *wholly owned* government corporations are required by default to comply with federal procurement policies and procedures.[26] In addition, the FAR stipulates that *wholly owned* government corporations are also subject to the Property Act.[27] These procurement and acquisition regulations therefore do not necessarily apply to *mixed-ownership* GOVCORPs, unless so stated under their charters.

With regard to personnel management requirements, many Title 5 provisions apply to both wholly owned and mixed-ownership GOVCORPs, though several important provisions specifically exclude either one or both.[28] For example, provisions

---

risks; to cap the liability faced by commercial participants in the nuclear power industry; and to obligate Congress to revisit liability compensation above the cap, in the event of a highly consequential nuclear incident. To the extent that the Price-Anderson Act does apply, that means first that some fraction of catastrophic liability risk would need to be insured pursuant to the terms of the Act; and second, in the event of a catastrophe, Congress would then be on the hook to consider and execute plans for additional compensation, to the extent needed.

[24] Kosar, 2011.

[25] Pub. L. 93-400, 41 U.S.C. §§ 401 et seq.

[26] The Office of Federal Procurement Policy Act has authority over executive agencies, which, within the act, are defined to include "a wholly owned Government corporation fully subject to the provisions of [the GCCA]" (31 U.S.C. § 403[1][D]).

[27] The FAR has authority over federal agencies, including executive agencies, which the act defines as including wholly owned government corporations listed in the GCCA (48 C.F.R. § 2.101).

[28] Section 105 of Title 5 defines *executive agency* as including government corporations. In turn, Title 5 defines a GOVCORP as "a corporation owned or controlled by the Government of the United States." Title 5 also defines

governing classification and general schedule pay rates apply to wholly owned GOV-CORPs but not mixed-ownership GOVCORPs.[29] Neither wholly owned nor mixed-ownership GOVCORPs are subject to the senior executive service or performance appraisal system provisions.[30]

Given the foregoing, wholly owned GOVCORPs tend by default to be more subject to government personnel and procurement rules than do mixed-ownership GOV-CORPs. This being said, it is always possible for Congress to exempt a GOVCORP from these administrative burdens through its charter, and TVA and OPIC are both examples of wholly owned GOVCORPs that do enjoy related exemptions.

As a practical matter, it is not clear how many GOVCORPs actually have these sorts of exemptions written into their charters. Note, however, that at least one commentator, when writing about GOVCORPs generally, asserted that "many are exempted from civil service rules regarding employee pay and tenure," and that they also tend to be able to "buy and sell assets without complying with federal procurement and disposal regulations."[31]

Without resolving the ambiguity, what seems clear is that the rationale for forming a GOVCORP often involves allowing the organization "to run on business-like principles." By extension, exemption from some aspects of government personnel management, procurement, and contracting rules could often be consistent with the same rationale.

GOVCORPs Can Transition to Private Corporations

Because GOVCORPs combine aspects of a government agency and private corporations, there is flexibility to transition to a different model. One example is the U.S. Enrichment Corporation (USEC), which transitioned from a GOVCORP to a private corporation in 1998 but has maintained a close relationship with the government through the leasing of facilities and through its involvement in the Megatons to Megawatts program with the Russian government. In April 1997, USEC entered into an executive agent memorandum of understanding with the Department of State and DOE. The memorandum stipulated that USEC would continue to serve as the executive agent in the government-to-government agreement between Russia and the United States concerning the sale of low-enriched uranium derived from highly enriched uranium in former Soviet warheads. In 2000, President Bill Clinton issued an executive order stipulating that all sales between the Russian government and USEC under the

---

the term *government-controlled corporations*, which specifically excludes wholly owned GOVCORPs. See 5 U.S.C. § 103.

[29] See 5 U.S.C. § 5102(a)(1)(A)(i) and 5 U.S.C. § 5331(a). An example is the Federal Deposit Insurance Corporation (FDIC), a mixed-ownership GOVCORP, which is not subject to classification provisions (*Dockery v Federal Deposit Insurance Corp.*, 64 M.S.P.R. 458, 460–462 [1994]).

[30] 5 U.S.C. § 3132(a)(1) and 5 U.S.C. § 4301(1)(i).

[31] Froomkin, 1995.

program must be specifically licensed by the Department of Treasury following an interagency review.[32] In this case, the organizational model can change but the nature of a private corporation's mission can place the organization under more government management than is typical in the general private sector.

Federally Chartered Private Corporation

Despite their title, federally chartered private corporations may also offer another way to blend some of the features of a private-sector organization and a government organization. A typical private-sector corporation is organized under the business corporation laws of a particular state, capitalized by private investors (e.g., stockholders), and set up to carry out a commercial purpose (e.g., to create revenue through business activities). The stockholders of a private corporation own the entity and its assets and are represented by an elected board of directors who exercise fiduciary oversight of the corporation and who hire and fire the CEO. By definition, a traditional business corporation is a profit-seeking entity—it exists to pool capital from a group of equity investors in order to facilitate the pursuit of a commercial enterprise. Note that the initial stage of organizing and launching a new corporation is usually begun by private parties (i.e., not the government). Although the charter of a new corporation includes some basic defining parameters for the organization, many of those defining parameters are already set out under the general business corporation laws of each state, and those parameters do not vary across individual corporations formed within a given state.

In contrast, some private corporations are federally chartered, and these are initially formed by an act of Congress. For our purposes, we define a PRIVCORP as a federally chartered, profit-seeking entity, created for a national goal or interest, and pooling capital from a group of equity investors to facilitate the pursuit of a commercial enterprise.

In general, PRIVCORPs are distinguished from GOVCORPs in that the former are owned and operated entirely in the private sector and compete directly in the market. Broadly speaking, a PRIVCORP is a category of organization that falls midway between a traditional private corporation and a GOVCORP. To clarify, if you start with a PRIVCORP and then take away its federal charter status, what you are left with is a privately owned, for-profit enterprise, organized in the corporate form and subject to the oversight of a board of directors. Superficially, at least, little remains to distinguish such an entity from any other for-profit corporation. However, if instead you start with a PRIVCORP and then take away private ownership (i.e., by making the entity wholly owned by the U.S. government), then it becomes difficult to distinguish that entity from a GOVCORP—defined, as noted above, as an organization formed and owned by the government, structured by federal charter, subject to some level of federal oversight, but carrying out a commercial activity, and with some of the governance attributes of a private corporation. As we describe in some detail below, the

---

[32] USEC, undated.

federal charter and federal mission of a PRIVCORP result in some important organizational features that are distinctive and not otherwise typical of private-sector corporations more generally.

Congressional Charter

Most private corporations are chartered under the business corporation laws of individual states; however, the federal government also has the authority to charter corporations when Congress deems this "necessary and proper."[33] Because Congress writes a unique, enacting charter document for each PRIVCORP, Congress establishes the basic mission and functions of the organization and determines its basic structural characteristics as well (e.g., the size and composition of its board).[34] Congress may also specify financial reporting requirements for the PRIVCORP to Congress and executive bodies, which would otherwise not typically apply; define specific powers and responsibilities as basic features of the PRIVCORP; and establish a specific relationship between the PRIVCORP and designated agencies and programs of the U.S. government. Because a federally chartered corporation is not formed under the business corporation laws of any specific state, such laws tend to apply its governance structure only to the extent that Congress so designates in its federal charter. Overall, PRIVCORPs are typically chartered with the intention of specifically separating them from a GOVCORP designation. To avoid the control mechanisms of the GCCA, Congress purposely designates these federally chartered private corporations as "*not* agencies or establishments of the United States government" within their statutes.[35]

Direct Oversight and the Roles of the President and Congress

As a private entity, a PRIVCORP is typically subject to the direct oversight of a board of directors, which represents the stockholders. Generally, the board is responsible for providing fiduciary oversight, hiring and firing the CEO, and providing high-level, strategic management.[36] As to the role of the President and Congress in a PRIVCORP, their direct corporate powers and duties are typically fairly limited and are defined by the federal charter that enacts its creation.

---

[33] This power was validated in the Supreme Court's ruling in *McCulloch v Maryland* (1819) in which the federal charter of the Second Bank was held to be constitutional under the "necessary and proper" clause within Article I.

[34] Note that, in contrast to an ordinary private-sector corporation, a federally chartered private corporation is typically construed as being empowered "to perform only those functions assigned to it in its enabling legislation" (GAO, 2008, p. 15-73). For example, the courts have enforced the charter limits on the functions of PRIVCORPs in several cases involving government-sponsored entities (GSEs). See *Association of Data Processing Service Organization, Inc. v Federal Home Loan Bank Board*, 568 F. 2d 478 (6th Cir. 1977); *Arnold Tours, Inc. v Camp*, 472 F. 2d 427 (1st Cir. 1972).

[35] *Lebron v Nat'l R.R. Passenger Corp.*, 513 U.S. 374, 390 (1995).

[36] Note that some commentators have argued that boards of private corporations are frequently "captured" by their CEOs in practice, such that the boards do not really perform effective oversight of management on behalf of stockholders. See, e.g., Elson, 1996, pp. 156–164.

Funding, Financial Management Oversight, and Borrowing Authority

The organizations in the PRIVCORP category tend to share many of the features and characteristics of other private-sector corporations, including for-profit status, limited liability for the stockholders, and private-sector business accounting and business finance practices. Although Congress could write an explicit charter provision to give such an organization special access to credit through the U.S. government, these entities are privately held corporations by their nature, and their debt and obligations are not generally backed by the full faith and credit of the United States. However, some PRIVCORPs have been informally viewed as being implicitly backed by the U.S. government—a perception that has sometimes made credit cheaper for them to obtain but that has also sometimes been associated with episodes of financial scandal.

Several of the best-known PRIVCORPs are the GSEs (e.g., Fannie Mae) that are devoted to addressing gaps in private-sector credit markets. The GSEs are all financial service organizations that provide loan financing to different sectors of the U.S. economy. Their liabilities are not guaranteed by the U.S. government, notwithstanding the perception among many that they are. The GSEs are examples of organizations that exist to fulfill a commercial purpose, but one in which the government also has a public policy interest—namely, in ensuring that credit financing is readily available for certain kinds of basic activities within the U.S. economy.[37]

Role of Stakeholders

The primary mode of stakeholder engagement in a PRIVCORP is through the representation of stockholders by a board of directors. Again, the directors are traditionally elected by stockholders as in any private-sector corporation, and the directors represent the stockholders both in fiduciary oversight and in the hiring and firing of the CEO. Although there are many other stakeholder groups that arguably have an interest in the operations of a private corporation (e.g., labor, customers, communities, state and local government), none of these would typically be represented on the board. The same would ordinarily be true of a PRIVCORP, unless Congress specifically chooses to write board representation for other stakeholder groups into the organization's charter.

As in the case of a GOVCORP, many other forms of stakeholder engagement that might be undertaken by a PRIVCORP are not likely to be dictated by its basic charter, although again, in principle, Congress could write charter provisions to compel a PRIVCORP to undertake other, specific stakeholder engagement activities (e.g., advisory boards, public awareness and education campaigns, etc.).

Ownership of Entity

As defined here, PRIVCORPs are entities completely owned by their private stockholders.

---

[37] See Kosar, 2007.

Regulatory Obligations

A traditional for-profit corporation formed under state law is subject to the corporate regulatory authority of the state in which it is formed, as per the business corporation statute of that state. Moreover, to the extent that that corporation issues equity securities, it may also be subject to SEC regulation. Moreover, relevant commercial activities may bring it under the authority of corresponding federal regulatory agencies, thus making it subject to the rules imposed by those agencies. Thus, PRIVCORPs that issue registered securities to the public are subject to SEC regulation; PRIVCORPs that engage in electricity-generating activities that fall within the ambit of Federal Energy Regulatory Commission (FERC) authority will be subject FERC regulation; PRIV-CORPs that operate airplanes and trains may be subject to the relevant regulations of the Federal Aviation Administration (FAA) and FRA, for example. Note that Congress has latitude when writing the charter of a PRIVCORP to stipulate additional forms of federal regulation that specifically apply, or to exempt the PRIVCORP from specific areas of regulation.

Legal Liabilities

Though Congress creates PRIVCORPs to serve a national goal or interest, they are nevertheless subject to the general laws of the states in which they conduct business, including laws pertaining to the acquisition and transfer of property, the collection of debts, and civil liability. PRIVCORPs can therefore typically sue and be sued and do not enjoy sovereign immunity for any torts that they commit.

Personnel Management, Procurement, and Contracting Mechanisms

Because they are private-sector organizations, PRIVCORPs are not generally subject to government administrative constraints in procurement, contracting, personnel management, or budgeting.

Independent Government Agency

Still another avenue for blending some of the features of a traditional government organization with those of a private-sector organization involves the establishment of a government agency. Although bound by a more formal set of regulations, responsibilities, and authorities, government agencies overall may comprise a wide variety of organizational structures in terms of placement and lines of authority. For example, agencies can be created in existing executive departments, and these can take varying forms, such as bureaus, program offices, services, and administrations; they may be created through executive order or congressional charter.

DOE itself contains program offices, operations offices, government-owned contractor-operated facilities, power marketing administrations (PMAs), and other administrative organizations. Many of these have greater or lesser independence in the way that they operate, in their executive and legislative oversight, and in their financing mechanisms. Notably, one of the PMAs, the BPA, was specifically cited by the BRC as a possible example to emulate for the nuclear waste organization. The BPA is described in detail in Appendix A and has characteristics of the typical IGA described below, except that it generates its own revenue and does not receive congressional appropriations.

As with the other organizational models, there is no formal, all-purpose statutory or judicial definition of an independent agency, although there are some basic, agreed-upon characteristics.[38] Independent agencies themselves have varied in purpose from regulatory bodies to overseers of specific agendas.[39] Today, the federal government includes around 88 independent agencies operating separately from executive departments.[40] What follows is a description of the typical characteristics of an IGA.

Congressional Charter

In general, Congress establishes an IGA through enacting legislation, with a narrower set of defined responsibilities than an executive department. Typically designed to be insulated from temporal political influence, these agencies enjoy a statutory grant of authority that defines the specific responsibilities, jurisdiction, and scope of authority of each.

Direct Oversight and the Roles of the President and Congress

The most common governing and executive structure for an IGA is a multimember board or commission, although several have only a single administrator.[41] In IGAs with a commission or board that serves as the chief executive and governing authority, these are typically appointed by the President and then confirmed by the Senate.[42] To maintain the objectivity of these IGAs, Congress typically includes variations of the following statutory arrangements with regard to their governance practices: bipartisan split in board member appointments, if applicable; fixed terms for the board members

---

[38] Breger and Edles, 2000, p. 1135.

[39] The concept of an independent agency at the federal level began with the establishment of the Interstate Commerce Commission (ICC) by Congress in the late 19th century. The ICC quickly gained independent power and authority to execute its mission, with limited ability for the executive office to affect the leadership or policies of the organization. Using the ICC as an example, the Progressive Era and New Deal brought about a multitude of independent agencies, despite controversy concerning their constitutionality (Breger and Edles, 2000, pp. 1132, 1116).

[40] GAO, 2009, pp. 11–13.

[41] For example, the board of governors of the Federal Reserve System has seven members appointed by the President (with the advice and consent of the Senate), whereas NASA has an administrator appointed by the President (with the advice and consent of the Senate). However, the U.S. Postal Service (USPS) has a board of governors appointed by the President (with the advice and consent of the Senate), who then appoints the Postmaster General.

[42] Note that the "boards" in these agencies tend to differ from those of a GOVCORP or PRIVCORP in that an agency "board" will often serve as the collective CEO of the agency, while, in a GOVCORP or PRIVCORP, the board of directors usually serves to appoint and monitor a CEO.

and chairperson positions; and limited removal procedures of governing persons as executed by the executive or legislative branches.[43]

IGAs have a fair amount of leeway in exercising their own policymaking and enforcement authority, although they may still take direction from the President. Most important, the bounds of an IGA's authority and jurisdiction are defined by its enacting statute. However, the U.S. Supreme Court has established that federal agencies, when their subject matter is "technical and complex," can have wide latitude in interpreting their own enacting statutes, although the typically inserted statutory phrase "to the maximum extent possible" still obligates them to fulfill their statutory obligations to "the extent that it is feasible or possible."[44]

Funding, Financial Management Oversight, and Borrowing Authority

The majority of IGAs receive their funding from direct appropriations. Depending on the enabling legislation, each IGA's budget and financial plans are either subject to OMB approval or given a waiver to submit their budgets directly to Congress to further insulate them from presidential pressure. Under the latter, OMB and the administration may still offer comments, but Congress may ultimately approve the budget without OMB clearance. IGAs may borrow from the Department of Treasury, and these debts are backed by the full faith and credit of the federal government.

Some IGAs, however, are self-funded or both. For example, USPS is a self-funded IGA and receives no appropriations (other than those for revenue waived on free and reduced-rate mail for the blind and on overseas voting materials for U.S. elections). All expenses incurred by USPS are paid for through the Postal Service Fund, which is a revolving fund consisting of revenues from postal and non-postal services, the appropriations previously discussed, interest earned on investments made by USPS, and other receipts and obligations of USPS. The NRC serves as an additional example of a partly self-funded agency. It receives fees from utilities to cover the costs of licensing activities but also receives direct appropriations from Congress to support defense and other national-level safety and research and development (R&D) functions.

Role of Stakeholders

In general, stakeholders involve various constituent groups interested in the subject matter for which the IGA has responsibility. IGAs may create advisory boards, in compliance with the Federal Advisory Committee Act, representing affected or interested parties, although these boards rarely have any formal governance or enforcement power. Other opportunities for stakeholder engagement would typically depend on

---

[43] Verkuil, 1988, p. 259.

[44] *Aluminum Co. of America v Central Lincoln Peoples' Utility Dist.*, 467 U.S. 380, 390 (1984); *Fund for Animals vs. Babbitt*, 903 F. Supp. 96, 107 (D.D.C. 1995), amended, 967 F. Supp. 6 (D.D.C. 1997) (citing *Doe v Board of Educ.*, 9 F. 3d 455, 460 [6th Cir. 1993]).

informal political channels, notice-and-comment rulemaking, and formal adjudication processes (where applicable).

Ownership of Entity

IGAs are wholly government owned and operated. They typically hold authority over a specific mission set or regulatory area.

Regulatory Obligations

As a government entity, an IGA is subject to OMB oversight, regulations applicable to federal employees, and those regulations set forth in the statute by which it was created. Certain activities may also fall under the regulatory purview of other government agencies. Occasionally, Congress may create a separate, independent entity with the sole purpose of determining compliance with congressional statutes and regulations of the agency in question, as through the creation of a pertinent Office of Inspector General. For example, the Postal Regulatory Commission deals solely with the activities of USPS, playing a large role in rate-setting and oversight of postal activities.

Legal Liabilities

Depending on the mission set of the IGA, Congress may stipulate specific liability requirements within the charter. For example, NASA must "consider, ascertain, adjust, determine, settle, and pay, on behalf of the United States" any claim for $25,000 or less for "bodily injury, death, or damage to or loss of real or personal property" that resulted from NASA carrying out its congressionally stipulated functions.[45] If a claim is greater than $25,000 and considered "meritorious" by NASA, it must report the situation to Congress for consideration. NASA is also authorized to provide liability insurance for any user of a space vehicle to cover injury to third-party persons or property. Overall, however, IGAs are subject to sovereign immunity and FTCA limits on vulnerability to civil suit.

Personnel Management, Procurement, and Contracting Mechanisms

Independent and semi-autonomous government agencies, unless specifically stipulated within their charters or public law, must abide by federal personnel management and civil service law requirements, including those under the Office of Labor-Management Standards (OLMS) and the Occupational Safety and Health Administration (OSHA). An example of an exception from federal civil service laws is USPS, which is federally mandated to give its employees compensation and benefits that are comparable to those in the private sector. The enabling legislation for an IGA may also exempt a portion of that agency's employees from certain civil service laws under Title 5, as illustrated by a NASA charter provision that allows the agency to appoint up to 425

---

[45] See Section 20113 (m)(1) of the National Aeronautics and Space Act of 1958, Pub. L. 111-314.

"scientific, engineering, and administrative personnel . . . without regard to [Title 5 Chapter 51 and subchapter III of Chapter 52] laws."[46]

The FARS (codified in Title 48) dictates how federal agencies procure goods and services and form and administer contracts. Some IGAs, however, have been exempted, either within their statutes or public law, and they create their own procurement regulations. For independent agencies, this includes USPS and FAA, as well as NASA to some extent.

Differences and Similarities of the Organizational Models

Having outlined some of the basic characteristics of the GOVCORP model, the PRIVCORP model, and the IGA model, one basic question that follows is, what are the key points of similarity and difference across these organizational models?

As shown in the first row of Table 3.1, all three organizational models find their origins in legislative acts of Congress. That means that, in each case, Congress specifically has to act to define the mission of each new organization, thereby determining many of its attributes. By extension, Congress also has the opportunity to deviate from the prototypical characteristics of an organizational model whenever it writes the enabling legislation for an IGA, PRIVCORP, or GOVCORP.

Thus, for example, although some of the prototypical features of a GOVCORP and of an IGA tend to differ (for example, in regard to budgeting, supervisory structures, and administrative requirements), Congress has the ability, in any given case, to craft a more or less "tailored" solution to a particular problem. By implication, the specific design choices that Congress makes in setting up a new organization may be at least as important as the broad categorical distinctions summarized in Table 3.1 in determining what the new organization will really look like and how it will function.

One of the chief points of distinction in Table 3.1 involves the concept of *ownership*. A PRIVCORP is privately owned (i.e., by stockholders), while an IGA is government owned. By comparison, a GOVCORP can either be wholly government owned or have a mixed-ownership structure with both government and private equity holders. These differences are important. Private ownership tends to be linked to a for-profit business orientation, to the payment of dividends to the owners from net operating surpluses (i.e., profits), and to a supervisory structure that emphasizes efficiency in the conduct of business. These can all be desirable attributes for an organization to have, at least in some circumstances. However, government ownership tends to be linked to a nonprofit orientation; to an emphasis on mission and public accountability (rather than on net operating surpluses); and to a supervisory structure designed to ensure political accountability, rather than stockholder accountability. These too can be desirable attributes in some circumstances.

---

[46] Pub. L. 111-314, § 20113(b)(1).

A related and important point of distinction across the organizational categories involves *board governance.* PRIVCORPs and (most) GOVCORPs have boards of directors, which serve as the primary oversight authorities for their organizations. In the PRIVCORP model, the board is typically elected by stockholders, has a corresponding fiduciary responsibility to monitor the business, and hires and fires the CEO. In a GOVCORP, the board is usually appointed by the President, has a fiduciary responsibility to monitor the organization (consistent with its charter-defined mission), and hires and fires the CEO.

There are significant differences between these various boards, but so too are there similarities. Board governance is a way of simultaneously insulating the executive management of an organization from outside interference and ensuring that key stakeholders are represented in oversight. By implication, board governance tends to be associated with independence of management. But it is also associated with stakeholder engagement because the constituencies represented on the board have direct access to, and authority over, top executives.[47]

In contrast with the foregoing, IGAs do not have fiduciary boards in the same way that PRIVCORPs and GOVCORPs do. Rather, many IGAs have a commission-style executive structure, in which the top executive authority within the IGA is itself divided among several people. Given that the top executive or executives in an IGA are typically appointed by and report directly to the President, they likely tend to be subject to more immediate supervision and oversight by executive branch and congressional authorities. The latter implies less independence and more political accountability.

A few other key distinctions across the three organizational models deserve mention. Both *financing mechanisms* and *administrative requirements* (personnel management, procurement, and contracting) tend to diverge across the models, such that PRIVCORPs tend to be least burdened by government administrative rules and financing mechanisms, while IGAs tend to be the most burdened. GOVCORPs tend to more closely resemble PRIVCORPs than IGAs on this dimension. By extension, some of the key features that tend to go along with PRIVCORP or GOVCORP status include revenue models that do not depend on congressional appropriations or approvals, accounting and audit practices that are more closely related to private-sector norms than to government norms, and (for most PRIVCORPs and at least some GOVCORPs) freedom from procurement and personnel requirements that broadly apply to IGAs. Again, the implication is that PRIVCORPs and GOVCORPs will tend to be somewhat more independent, more internally flexible, and more oriented toward commercial ventures than their traditional agency counterparts.[48] All these features can

---

[47] Note particularly that, in a GOVCORP, Congress has considerable latitude in designing a board structure to maximize the engagement of key stakeholder groups by assigning them direct representation on the board.

[48] None of which is to say that an independent agency could not be set up by Congress to have some of the same characteristics in terms of greater flexibility, "self-sustaining" financing, and other features. It is merely to say that

sometimes be advantages, depending on the function of a particular organization and the context in which it will operate.

Finally, another point of distinction across the three categories deserves note. Organizational *liability* (particularly in the sense of being vulnerable to tort lawsuits) is another attribute that distinguishes PRIVCORPs and GOVCORPs from IGAs, in that the latter typically fall in the scope of sovereign immunity and the FTCA, while the former usually do not. This being said, the word *liability* is also sometimes used in a broader sense to refer to the ultimate financial responsibility for debts or obligations incurred by an organization (as in the case of bankruptcy or some other catastrophic event).

There are two related points to consider here. The first is that PRIVCORPs and GOVCORPs are not typically backed by the full faith and credit of the United States, other than as stipulated by Congress in a specific organizational charter. That has various implications for debt financing undertaken by those organizations and it represents a significant potential advantage for federal agencies in their ability to borrow money. The second point, however, is that, for any organization that actually faces catastrophic liability in the course of fulfilling an important public policy function, there can sometimes be political pressure for government to become involved as an insurance backstop (and for taxpayers to shoulder the liability) in the context of an actual catastrophe.[49] Although the ex-ante legal parameters for this kind of government liability differ across PRIVCORPs, GOVCORPs, and IGAs, the political parameters for intervention after the fact may sometimes trump the law. In thinking about the most appropriate organizational design for an MDO, extralegal issues connected with the importance of debt financing, the potential for catastrophic liability, and the likely role of government as an insurance backstop of last resort could all be useful factors to consider.

Conclusions

The purpose of this chapter has been to describe and contrast several organizational models that could each be used to implement a new MDO. Because there is considerable flexibility within each, and latitude for Congress to tailor the structure of a corresponding organization to maximize its likelihood for success, it is really not possible to assess the advantages and disadvantages of these theoretical models. It is clear that any evaluation of the comparative merits of the different organizational models will need

---

that would be less prototypical of that category generally.

[49] In this regard, it is again worth noting that the Price-Anderson Act establishes exactly this kind of federal risk backstop for utilities involved in the nuclear power industry, and for related DOE facilities and subcontractors. In connection with any future MDO that Congress might establish, one threshold design question for Congress to consider would be whether (and how) the terms of the Price-Anderson Act should apply to the new entity.

to be contextual and will depend on the mission to be performed, on the performance goals of the MDO, and on the anticipated barriers that will need to be overcome.

In a vacuum, there is no objective answer to the question of whether a for-profit corporation or a nonprofit government entity is a "better" type of organization. Each has proven to be useful for different things. And historically, both have been employed with success in a variety of applications.

Because there is considerable latitude within each of the PRIVCORP, GOV-CORP, and IGA models, the specific MDO legislative choices that Congress makes within any one of these categories may be every bit as important to success as is the threshold decision of which model to pursue. It is probably fair to say that we could deliberately design an MDO likely to fail, using any of the three models, simply by making bad or self-defeating choices in some of the details (e.g., setting up a maladaptive governing board, an inadequate financing mechanism). It is more challenging to design an MDO likely to succeed. Doing so will very likely go beyond the basic choice of an organizational model to pinning down some key parameters within the model that are likely to affect its success.

Finally, there can sometimes be a recursive element in pairing a good organizational model with a clear plan for implementation. If stakeholder engagement is an important part of the MDO mission, then that seems likely to influence MDO operations and strategy in ways that might reflect back on optimal choices about the MDO's form of organization. Likewise, if the operational plan for the MDO involves outsourcing much of its function to contractors, then that too might influence what the best structural model for the MDO would be in helping to fulfill that operational plan. Again, in choosing the organizational model, one way to approach these sorts of considerations would be to pin them down as explicit assumptions. The assumptions can then help to ground the comparative assessment of benefits and drawbacks across organizational models and to support sensitivity testing connected with key details of implementation.

CHAPTER FOUR

Matching Organizational Models to Critical Organizational Attributes

Although there could be reasons for picking one organizational model over another on the basis of their characteristics, we discovered that more analysis was required with a focus on how well each of the models relates to what is desired in terms of the new MDO's operational performance. So, in this chapter we describe the complex and unique responsibilities of the new MDO, its performance goals, and the critical organizational attributes that will enable the MDO to achieve its goals. We then describe the concrete structural and procedural features in an organization's design that could produce these attributes and assess whether these features exist or could be built into one or more of the organizational models. Our analytic framework is shown in Figure 4.1.

Mission and Responsibilities

The mission of the new MDO includes management, storage, transportation and disposal of used fuel and defense high-level nuclear waste while protecting the safety and security of communities and the national interest. In fulfilling its mission, the MDO will undertake first-of-a-kind, complex, and long-term projects. The work will also involve extensive interaction with other entities, including Congress; federal agencies; tribal, state, and local governments; nongovernmental organizations; commer-

Figure 4.1
Framework for Linking Responsibilities, Performance Goals, Attributes, and Features

cial nuclear power generators; and advisory groups. The MDO's activities will require extensive engagement with the public as well.[1]

The responsibilities of the MDO can be broken down into those that are "core" (that is, central to the MDO's ability to fulfill its mission) and those that are "management and support." The principal elements of the MDO's mission and the core responsibilities that relate to each element are identified in Table 4.1. A notional view of the phasing of MDO's responsibilities over time is shown in Figure 4.2. In executing its core responsibilities, the MDO will be able to carry them out directly, contract for other entities to carry them out, or facilitate other entities' carrying them out. Depending on the means chosen for executing its core responsibilities, the MDO will have a greater or lesser role in funding such execution and in coordinating the activities of other entities that may share some of these responsibilities.

Core Responsibilities

The first undertaking of the MDO will be to identify and select sites for facilities to store commercial used fuel and to dispose of used fuel and defense high-level nuclear waste. Siting will be by far the most complex undertaking of the new organization and, as has been apparent during the past 30 years, one fraught with challenges and uncertainties in the natural and human environments.

Table 4.1
Core Responsibilities of the MDO

Elements of MDO Mission	Core Responsibilities
Provide consolidated storage capacity for used fuel	• Site facilities • Obtain licenses • Construct • Operate • Close and decommission
Facilitate safe and secure transportation of used fuel and defense high-level nuclear waste from utilities and government-operated sites to storage and disposition sites	• Plan and design routing • Certify cask designs • Develop safety and security procedures
Provide one or more facilities for disposal of used fuel and defense high-level waste	• Site facilities • Obtain licenses • Construct • Operate • Close and decommission
Plan and manage facility- and site-specific research, development, and demonstration activities	• Plan and manage research • Translate research into engineering design • Demonstrate in field

---

[1] The degree to which the new MDO will carry out these responsibilities "in house," use contractors, or facilitate the undertaking of some or all of these responsibilities by other entities will have to be decided in the context of determining the details of the MDO's design. For example, it may be possible for a public-private consortium to volunteer a site for regional storage, handling, and other related facilities; secure financing; apply for a license; and construct, operate, and close such facilities. Some have suggested that regional airport authorities offer a model for such a public-private consortium, even suggesting the integration of a repository with the other storage and handling facilities. See, for example, Forsberg, 2012.

Figure 4.2
A Notional View of the Phasing of the MDO's Responsibilities

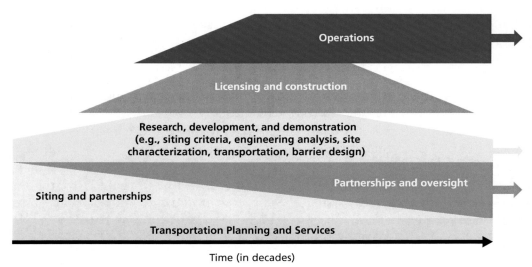

Operations

Licensing and construction

Research, development, and demonstration
(e.g., siting criteria, engineering analysis, site
characterization, transportation, barrier design)

Partnerships and oversight

Siting and partnerships

Transportation Planning and Services

Time (in decades)

RAND *MG1230-4.2*

For storage facilities and repository sites, the first step in site selection is to define the general system concept—what the facility will do, its size, its duration of operations, and anticipated regulatory standards that will apply to it. Defining the concept will provide local communities that might be considering hosting a facility a general idea of what they would be getting involved in. As outlined by the BRC, site identification will be facilitated if the MDO can develop some basic initial selection criteria. This would provide a first-order filter on the acceptability of a site. For a permanent geological repository, these criteria might include geologic and hydrologic conditions, historical seismic and volcanic activity, and possibly some social considerations such as proximity to population centers. Initial criteria for a consolidated storage facility are less obvious, but would likely also include geologic settings, transportation linkages, and social considerations such as proximity to communities with existing nuclear power plants.

A consent-based siting process, as called for by the BRC, will require extensive interaction with candidate site communities, which implies a number of responsibilities. It will be necessary to develop a formal process for engaging and interacting with communities and local, state, and tribal authorities. The process would be used to solicit expressions of interest for hosting sites and provide a forum for information sharing and negotiations. Interaction with candidate site communities will entail developing an education and public involvement program—communities will need to be accurately and comprehensively informed about what hosting a site will involve. This interaction will also involve designing incentives for local communities and states or tribes to consider and to accept a facility, as well as an active effort to encourage and solicit expressions of interest from candidate localities. Past experience suggests that the MDO will need flexibility in developing packages of incentives likely to appeal to each distinct community. As promising sites emerge, the MDO will need to negotiate agreements with communities, states, and tribes about such issues as size, duration (for centralized storage), options for expansion, and terms of commitment (including schedules for increasing degrees of commitment and penalties for backing out). Finally, the MDO will need to find the right middle ground between establishing a clear roadmap for achieving the siting with clear expectations without imposing inflexible deadlines that do not allow for unforeseen developments.

Once a site is selected, the entire enterprise of scientific and engineering research, analysis, design, and demonstration will be organized around the license application requirements set forth by the NRC and the environmental standards established and enforced by EPA. A key responsibility of the MDO will be to characterize the site, model the performance of the system (be it surface or underground storage or underground disposal), and submit a license application to the NRC. As noted earlier, for some storage and related facilities, an entity other than the MDO could be the licensee; in such a situation, the MDO would be involved in funding and play an integrating and coordinating role to ensure consistency across sites and efficiency within a national system. In either case, site characterization presents many opportunities for the implementing organization to engage with the local community and the broader public and to demonstrate transparency and openness as deeper understanding is gained about the particular strengths and weaknesses of a given site.

Beyond these responsibilities will be design and engineering of the facilities; interactions with federal, state, and local authorities in conducting thorough environmental security assessments; and monitoring of the environmental performance of the facilities and the networks for transporting used fuel. If the MDO is not the implementing organization, then its role will be to ensure that these activities have the benefit of full intergovernmental coordination and cooperation in review and regulatory matters, and full consistency with the principles of a consent-based, transparent, and science-based process.

The MDO will need to either manage the construction process itself or, more likely, procure the services of major engineering project management and construction firms to successfully implement these megaprojects. Once the facilities are built, the MDO will have a variety of responsibilities, including arranging transfer of title to the used fuel from the utilities to the MDO, planning and overseeing transport of the used fuel, and implementing environmental and security systems. For consolidated storage sites, the MDO will have the responsibility, eventually, to decommission them by either dismantling or selling the infrastructure, cleaning the site, and releasing the land. Again, the possibility exists that a regional public-private consortium or some other similar type of entity could be the licensee, constructor, and operator of a consolidated storage site, with the MDO playing a coordinating role. For either a storage facility or a geologic repository, the decision to close a site will require extensive analysis and public discussion because it could occur as long as 100 years after the facility was first opened.

Achieving the safe delivery of used fuel to consolidated storage facilities and to a final repository will require the MDO to carry out additional responsibilities, including planning for and designing transportation facilities and services; procuring trucks, rail cars, and containers; conducting public outreach, communication, and education to gain support from affected communities; and routing, scheduling, monitoring, and safeguarding shipments.

An MDO will also need to manage and fund research to support licensing and regulatory compliance and to deal with unforeseen events or circumstances. There is still more to be learned about what will be needed to store and dispose of used fuel and defense high-level nuclear waste; thus, the MDO will need to be responsible for developing new technologies, such as casks, backfill, and monitoring systems to bolster natural and engineered barriers likely to be employed at a given site.

Management and Support Responsibilities

For the core responsibilities to be fulfilled, the MDO also will have to carry out management and support responsibilities in a manner that ensures efficient and accountable operations. These include policy formulation and planning, management of relations with external entities, financial management, administrative management, and regulatory compliance. The effective performance of these foundational and cross-cutting responsibilities will be essential to building trust and confidence in the integrity of the MDO, exercising responsible stewardship of the financial and other authorities vested in the organization, and imbuing the culture of the organization with a focus on performance, transparency, and trust-building.

Performance Goals

In this section, we identify a set of performance goals for the MDO. The MDO will need to achieve these goals if it is to succeed in effectively managing and disposing of used fuel and defense high-level nuclear waste. These performance goals are based on our analysis in Chapter Two of the problems that arose with past organizational arrangements, as well as the responsibilities of the new MDO described in the previous section. In developing these goals, we also have drawn on past studies, the BRC report, and background papers prepared for the BRC.[2]

---

[2]   See BRC, 2012, pp. 5–8; AMFM, 1984, Part III; DOE, 2001, pp. 24–27. The BRC report distinguishes "core interests and objectives for U.S. waste management policy" from "core values and principles for a successful waste management program"; we have drawn from both in developing the set of performance goals we present here.

These performance goals take into account the inherent characteristics of used fuel and defense high-level nuclear waste that impose special burdens on how an MDO should carry out its functions. These include the unique and long-lived hazard that nuclear materials pose to human health and the environment, as well as the widespread public perception of that hazard. Storage and disposal solutions must be crafted with utmost attention to safety and security; ultimately, these solutions must last longer than any organizational enterprise—governmental or otherwise—that has ever existed. Moreover, because no permanent disposal solutions for used fuel and defense high-level nuclear waste have yet been implemented anywhere, a successful MDO will have to break new ground both technically and politically.

The key performance goals for an MDO are these:

- **Ensure that used-fuel and defense high-level nuclear waste management decisions meet the highest standards for safety and protection of human health and the environment.** The reason special storage and geological disposal facilities are needed for used fuel and defense high-level nuclear waste is to provide protection to humans and other life forms from exposure to these materials which continue to emit radiation harmful for hundreds of thousands of years. Consequently, it is essential that the MDO decisionmaking process be designed to ensure that sufficient investigation is undertaken to define confidently the health and safety protection requirements for the facilities and that the facilities be designed and constructed to meet these requirements. Achieving this goal requires that decisions be based on sound science and technical excellence. Aspiring to this goal is the central purpose of a storage and disposal facility program. This goal has applied to past nuclear waste management efforts and needs to continue to apply to all future efforts.

- **Achieve siting of storage and disposal facilities on the basis of informed consent of states, tribes, and local communities.** Because decisionmaking authority has largely been confined to federal government officials, a consistent theme in past efforts associated with managing spent nuclear fuel has been strong opposition from state governments. Beginning with the first repository plan in Lyons, Kansas, in the early 1970s and continuing through the Waste Isolation Pilot Plant (WIPP), the initial site candidates selected under the NWPA, efforts to develop a centralized storage (MRS) facility, and, of course, Yucca Mountain itself, every effort was severely hampered by forceful opposition from states and, in some cases, communities. The lesson learned from these experiences is that, in order to obtain local support and buy-in, states, tribes, and local communities need to have a substantive role in the decisionmaking process. Examples of the benefit of this approach include the success of WIPP only after DOE ceded substantial regulatory authority to the state, and the anticipated success of the consent-based site-selection process in Sweden.

- **Earn public trust and confidence in decisionmaking processes and results.** A critical element in the struggles associated with implementing the NWPA was that the public's trust and confidence in the integrity of the decisionmaking process eroded over time. Explicit decisions, such as DOE suspending efforts to develop a second repository in May 1986 and Congress declaring that Yucca Mountain be the only site considered for a repository in the NWPA amendments, as well as ongoing evidence of inconsistent priorities and poor management within DOE,[3] led the public to lose confidence that the federal decisionmakers were competent and fair. As confidence and trust continued to erode, it became increasingly difficult to gain public support for pursuing the effort.
- **Ensure cost-effectiveness of storage and disposal solutions.** An important goal for any program in the public or private sector is to deliver the desired results with the least expenditure of resources possible. In the case of storing and disposing of commercial used fuel, this goal is important because the effort has been and will continue to be funded by ratepayers of utilities generating electricity from nuclear plants. High storage and disposition costs will negatively affect affordability.

Critical Organizational Attributes

The MDO will need to be designed in a way that maximizes the ability of its leaders and personnel to achieve the performance goals stated above. The question thus arises, what organizational attributes will facilitate the achievement of those goals? Table 4.2 identifies the critical attributes that are associated with each of the performance goals.

In reading Table 4.2, it is important to note that some organizational attributes relate to more than one goal and thus appear more than once in the table. Each of the attributes identified in Table 4.2 is discussed in this section, including an explanation of its relevance to the performance goals. This discussion is organized in accordance with the performance goals with which the attributes are associated.

Ensure That Nuclear Waste Management Decisions Meet the Highest Standards for Public Safety and Protection of Human Health and the Environment

Because of the hazardous and long-lasting characteristics of nuclear waste discussed earlier, the MDO will need to have the capacity to place public interests in safety and security above narrower stakeholder interests, including financial interests. Having an explicit *public interest mission* can help ensure that the MDO weighs interests in this fashion.

Insulation from political control will enable the MDO to make decisions on the basis of long-term, objective, health and safety factors, rather than short-term political

---

[3]   GAO, 1993, 1994a, 1994b.

Table 4.2
Organizational Attributes Needed to Achieve Performance Goals

Performance Goal	Critical Organizational Attribute
Ensure that nuclear waste management decisions meet the highest standards for public safety and protection of human health and the environment	Public interest mission (i.e., mission to serve long-term public interests as highest priority)
	Insulation from political control
	Accountability to elected authorities and judicial authorities
	Technical capabilities to make science-based decisions that meet the highest standards for safety and human health and environmental protection
	Technical capabilities to conduct the scientific and engineering research, analysis, design, and demonstration and the environmental regulation compliance activities required for the license application process and to oversee and evaluate such work undertaken by contractors
	Organizational stability: durability of organization
	Organizational stability: consistency of policy direction
	Organizational stability: consistency of management
Achieve siting of storage and disposal facilities on the basis of informed consent of states, tribes, and local communities	Political credibility and influence to engage successfully with communities, states, and tribes in a consent-based siting process
	Ability to commit to providing monetary and nonmonetary incentives
	Clear mandate to make siting decisions and the associated legal capacity to enter into binding agreements with states, tribes, and local communities
	Technical capabilities to undertake site evaluation, selection, and planning
Earn public trust and confidence in decisionmaking processes and results	Transparent decisionmaking processes
	Insulation from political control
	Accountability to elected authorities and judicial authorities
	Technical capabilities to make science-based decisions that meet the highest standards for safety and human health and environmental protection
	Organizational stability: durability of organization
	Organizational stability: consistency of policy direction
	Organizational stability: consistency of management
Ensure cost-effectiveness of storage and disposal solutions	Management capabilities to plan and implement "megaprojects," either directly or through oversight and evaluation of contractors
	Legal capacity to procure services; purchase, lease, and dispose of land and other property; and hold title to spent fuel

considerations. Balancing insulation with *accountability* will enable those authorities with broad duties to protect the public to ensure that the MDO fulfills its public interest mission. *Technical capabilities* are essential to the MDO's competence with respect to making decisions regarding public safety and protection of health and the environment. The organization will need personnel with technical capabilities for conducting scientific and engineering activities, rigorously overseeing contractors performing such activities, and for ensuring regulatory compliance. The three elements of *organizational stability*—durability, policy consistency, and management consistency—are important for the MDO to be able to take a long-term view of safety and health and environmental protection matters and for programs intended to address these matters to be carried out consistently over a long period of time.

Achieve Siting of Storage and Disposal Facilities on the Basis of Informed Consent of States, Tribes, and Local Communities

As discussed in detail in the BRC final report, successful siting of storage, repository, and material-handling facilities will require a consent-based process.[4] Such a process will require negotiations between the MDO and states, tribes, and local communities that are potential site hosts. To negotiate successfully and elicit consent, the MDO will need both credibility and leverage, and it will need to be seen to the fullest extent possible as the final authority able to deliver a conclusive agreement on siting.

These requirements imply that the MDO will need to have enough connectedness to political authorities—what we refer to as *political credibility and influence*—that states, tribes, and local communities will be assured that the MDO will be able to prevent or mitigate political interference with a siting agreement. They also imply that the MDO will need to have the *ability to commit* to providing the monetary and non-monetary incentives that will be crucial to concluding agreements on siting; without this ability, the MDO will not be able to make credible and attractive offers in negotiations. In addition, the MDO will need to have a *clear mandate* to make siting decisions so that it will be seen as the final authority with which potential site hosts can come to an agreement and so that they will be motivated to engage with the MDO in negotiations. It will also need to have the associated *legal capacity to enter into binding agreements* with states, tribes, and local communities, so that it can conclude agreements without having to refer to other authorities.

Furthermore, as discussed earlier, siting is an extremely complex process. To successfully accomplish siting, and to do so in a way that builds public trust and confidence and elicits consent, the MDO will need to have the *technical capabilities* to

---

4   Implementing a consent-based process, in which the MDO's conduct is consistently open, transparent, and fair, will not, however, guarantee successful siting of storage and repository facilities. For a discussion of this point, see IAEA, 2007, pp. 45–46.

undertake site evaluation, selection, and planning, and all of the related and subsidiary technical tasks that those responsibilities imply.

Earn Public Trust and Confidence in Decisionmaking Processes and Results

Public trust in an organization consists of the belief that the organization will take public interests into account, and confidence exists when the public feels sure that the organization knows of its interests, is competent to act on that knowledge, and will keep its word.[5] Public trust and confidence cannot be conferred on the MDO at the time it is established; earning trust and confidence will depend primarily on the MDO's organizational behavior over time—that is, on demonstrating its trustworthiness through its actions.[6] Those actions will include engaging seriously and credibly in a consent-based siting process and communicating effectively and openly with the public. Subsequent to the siting process, whether the MDO or another organization is the licensee, the MDO will need to ensure that all activities carried out under the MDO's mission are demonstrative of its trustworthiness.

Certain organizational attributes can help the MDO to earn trust and confidence, however. *Transparent decisionmaking processes* are one important attribute because they will give the public the opportunity to see whether the MDO is taking their interests into account.[7] Such transparency will need to include communicating with the public credibly and in a timely way regarding decisionmaking procedures and their results. *Insulation from political control* will help the MDO to act on the basis of objectively defined long-term public interests and will help it to keep its word. Insulation will have to be balanced, though, with *accountability to elected and judicial authorities* that are charged with protecting public interests. In light of the uniquely hazardous nature of nuclear waste, public belief in the MDO's technical competence also will go a long way toward ensuring confidence in its decisions. Thus, the MDO will need to have *technical capabilities* to make science-based decisions that meet the highest standards for safety and protections of human health and the environment.[8]

Furthermore, *organizational stability* will be crucial to persuading the public that the MDO can and will keep its word—that its agreements with host communities

---

[5]   See La Porte and Metlay, 1996, p. 342.

[6]   Tuler and Kasperson emphasize that a new MDO will not enjoy social trust at the outset of its work and will likely have to function in the absence of trust for some time (Tuler and Kasperson, 2010, pp. 3, 8). See also SEAB, 1993, p. 41, which concludes that organizational behavior is "far more important" than organizational forms or structures for creating or inhibiting public trust and confidence.

[7]   Regarding the importance of transparency also for purposes of ensuring intergenerational equity, see National Academy of Public Administration, 1997, p. 8.

[8]   SEAB (1993), among others that have considered this issue, emphasizes the importance of technical and managerial competence, as well as science-based decisionmaking, for earning public trust and competence. Such competence and other measures to build trust and confidence will have to involve contractors, given the likely importance of their role in the work of an MDO (SEAB, 1993, p. 42).

will have staying power. Three distinct elements of organizational stability will be important for the MDO: institutional *durability*, *policy consistency*, and *management consistency*.

Durability will instill confidence that, given the long-lasting nature of nuclear waste, holding the MDO accountable will be feasible over a very long period time. Guaranteeing the MDO's endurance over the full life span of the materials it will manage is impossible. Thus, for potential organizational forms other than an IGA, contingency arrangements for MDO termination will need to be specified in the MDO's charter, including provisions for the reversion of title to materials to the U.S. government and for the disposition of facilities.

Policy consistency can help earn trust and confidence by reassuring the public that the MDO will faithfully adhere to its commitments over the long period of time and large scale of activity required to site, construct, and manage storage and disposal facilities.[9] Policy swings were a key factor undermining OCRWM's ability to earn trust and confidence. It should be noted, however, that, depending on the particular policies pursued and whether there might be benefits to changing policy, there may be trade-offs between policy stability and flexibility.[10]

Management consistency is closely linked to policy consistency because the former will help ensure the latter. Views of experts long involved in nuclear waste management matters are mixed on whether or not management turnover undermined the effectiveness of past organizational arrangements. Nevertheless, stability among the MDO's management cadre doubtless would be helpful in persuading the public that MDO leaders, because of their longevity, understand the public's interests and are committed to fulfilling the MDO's mission.

Ensure Cost-Effectiveness of Storage and Disposal Solutions

To ensure cost-effectiveness, the MDO will need *management capabilities* of the types and quality needed to plan and implement so-called megaprojects—that is, infrastructure development projects of an extremely large scale and high cost and to which there will be intense public attention.[11] This will be particularly important in the phases of the MDO's work following siting activities. The MDO also will need the *legal capacity* and flexibility to cost-effectively procure services and purchase, lease, and dispose of land and other property. The nature of the MDO's mission requires as well that it have the legal capacity to hold title to both used fuel and defense high-level nuclear waste. Licensees other than the MDO will require similar capacities consistent with the scope and nature of their undertaking.

---

[9]   See La Porte and Keller, 1996, p. 538.

[10]   On this trade-off, see McCubbins, Noll, and Weingast, 1989, p. 440.

[11]   Merrow, 2011.

Structural and Procedural Features and Analysis of Organizational Models

In many respects, the MDO will develop the critical organizational attributes discussed in the previous section through the manner in which it conducts its activities over time and through the direction set and values communicated by its leadership. But to varying extents the attributes also can be produced by the structural and procedural features of the organization's design. Some of these features are inherent to a particular organizational model, while others are not. In some cases, these features can be built into the organizational model in order to produce the attributes.

Table 4.3 provides examples of structural and procedural features that can produce each of the critical organizational attributes. This is not a comprehensive list of features, but it includes those that are most fundamental to the organization's design. Many of these can—and, indeed, would need to—be written into legislation enabling the MDO.

For each of the structural and procedural features, we denote whether it is inherent to each of the organizational models (indicated by "Yes(I)") or whether it is possible to build it in (indicated by "Yes(B)"). In the cases where the features can be built into the organizational model, it is important to note that some will be practically and politically more difficult than others, even where it is possible in principle to do so. For example, Table 4.3 shows that, in principle, under any of the three models, it is possible to provide for assured and adequate funding for the MDO without reliance on annual appropriations, but we do not mean to suggest that doing so will be practically or politically easy.

The discussion of the structural and procedural features that follows is organized in accordance with the attribute with which they are associated. Because the features produce the critical organizational attributes in different ways and there are multiple features for each attribute, one cannot conclude from Table 4.3 alone whether one organizational model is superior to another.

Public Interest Mission

Having a public interest mission is a critical attribute for the MDO. This will ensure that the MDO is oriented toward serving the long-term public interest as its highest value. Creating this attribute will require enshrining that mission in the enabling legislation or charter. This could be done under either the IGA or GOVCORP model but would be conceptually inconsistent with a for-profit PRIVCORP, which, by definition, would have to value shareholder interests above other interests.

Accountability

Judicial review of compliance with the MDO's enabling legislation or charter is possible under each of the three models. Public accountability can also be achieved through

Table 4.3
Structural and Procedural Features That Produce Organizational Attributes Identified in Table 4.2

Critical Organizational Attribute	Structural and Procedural Feature	Can the Model Have the Feature?		
		PRIVCORP	GOVCORP	IGA
Public interest mission (i.e., mission to serve long-term public interests as highest priority)	Enact in legislation establishing MDO	No	Yes(I)	Yes(I)
Accountability to elected authorities and judicial authorities	Nomination role for President and Senate confirmation for MDO leader	No	No	Yes(I)
	Nomination role for President and Senate confirmation for governance board of directors	No	Yes(B)	Yes(I)
	Specify congressional oversight provisions in enabling legislation/charter, potentially including designating committees that will have oversight responsibility	No	Yes(B)	Yes(I)
	Specify in enabling legislation/charter that states will have a regulatory role with respect to sited facilities (for the protection of human health and the environment)	Yes(B)	Yes(B)	Yes(B)
	Create independent IG with public reporting responsibilities	No	Yes(B)	Yes(B)
Transparent decisionmaking processes	Notification and participation requirements for siting process and notice and comment–type procedures for major decisions written into enabling legislation/charter	Yes(B)*	Yes(B)	Yes(B)
	Public-meeting requirement written into enabling legislation/charter	Yes(B)	Yes(B)	Yes(B)
	Create independent IG, with public reporting responsibilities	No	Yes(B)	Yes(B)
Political credibility and influence to engage successfully with communities, states, and tribes in a consent-based siting process	Presidential nomination and Senate confirmation for MDO leader	No	No	Yes(I)
	Presidential nomination and Senate confirmation for governance board	No	Yes(B)	Yes(I)[a]
	Designated coordinating role in executive branch interagency process, to facilitate consensus and cooperation among agencies having regulatory roles in siting, transportation, and related matters	No	No	Yes(B)
	MDO representation in interagency group led by Domestic Policy Council, OMB, or Secretary of Energy to facilitate consensus and cooperation among agencies having regulatory roles in siting, transportation, and related matters	Yes(B)*	Yes(B)	Yes(I)
	Governance board whose members represent interests likely to be aligned with those of states, tribes, and local communities	Yes(B)*	Yes(B)	Yes(B)
	Advisory board whose members represent interests likely to be aligned with those of states, tribes, and local communities	Yes(B)	Yes(B)	Yes(B)

Table 4.3—Continued

Critical Organizational Attribute	Structural and Procedural Feature	Can the Model Have the Feature?		
		PRIVCORP	GOVCORP	IGA
Insulation from political control	Multimember board or commission variation of governance model, with fixed and staggered terms for board members or commissioners and party-affiliation balance requirement	Not needed	Not needed	Yes(B)
	Fixed, lengthy term for the MDO administrator or board/commission chairperson, with a limit on the number of terms the administrator/chairperson may serve (e.g., one term, one term plus one renewal)	Not needed	Not needed	Yes(B)
	Limit grounds for removal of the MDO administrator or board/commission chairperson (e.g., for-cause removal, with causes specified)	Not needed	Not needed	Yes(B)
	Limit review of siting decisions to judicial authorities (i.e., no review by President or by other executive branch authorities, except in the context of their exercise of specified regulatory functions)	Yes (I)	Yes(I)	Yes(B)
	Assured and adequate funding without dependence on annual appropriations	Yes(B)	Yes(B)	Yes(B)
Organizational stability: durability of organization	Assured and adequate funding without dependence on annual appropriations	Yes(B)	Yes(B)	Yes(B)
	U.S. government backing of debt	Yes(B)*	Yes(B)	Yes(I)
	Ability to adapt to changing functional emphasis over time	Yes(I)	Yes(B)	Yes(B)*
Organizational stability: consistency of policy direction	Substantive qualifications for MDO leader specified in enabling legislation/charter	Yes(B)*	Yes(B)	Yes(B)
	Limit (in legislation) number or percentage of political appointees	Not needed	Not needed	Yes(B)
	Multimember board or commission variation of governance model, with fixed and staggered terms for board members or commissioners, and party-affiliation balance requirement	Not needed	Not needed	Yes(B)
	Fixed, lengthy term for MDO leader	No	No	Yes(B)
	Preclude presidential review of MDO's major decisions, including siting	Yes(I)	Yes(B)	Yes(B)

Table 4.3—Continued

Critical Organizational Attribute	Structural and Procedural Feature	Can the Model Have the Feature?		
		PRIVCORP	**GOVCORP**	**IGA**
Organizational stability: consistency of management	Multimember board or commission variation of governance model, with fixed and staggered terms for board members or commissioners; under this variation, the board or commission chair would stand in place of the MDO administrator with respect to other features noted in this table	Not needed	Not needed	Yes(B)
	Fixed, lengthy term for MDO administrator, with a limit on the number of terms the administrator may serve (e.g., one term, one term plus one renewal)	No	No	Yes(B)
	Limit grounds for removal of the MDO administrator (e.g., for-cause removal, with causes specified)	No	No	Yes(B)
	Limit (in legislation) number or percentage of political appointees	Not needed	Not needed	Yes(B)
Clear mandate to make siting decisions and the associated legal capacity to enter into binding agreements with states, tribes, and local communities	Enshrine mandate and legal capacity in enacting legislation/charter	Yes(B)	Yes(B)	Yes(B)
Ability to commit to providing monetary and nonmonetary incentives	Assured up-front funding resources that can be used to pay for incentives, and discretion to allocate those resources, subject to auditing but not merit review of allocation decisions	Yes(B)	Yes(B)	Yes(B)
	Direct involvement in interagency process that would produce decisions on nonmonetary incentives, such as siting of unrelated federal facilities (for purposes of economic development and employment generation), and on provision of federal grants for programs related to storage and disposal siting (such as development of emergency response capabilities)[b]	No	No	Yes(I)
	MDO representation in interagency group to produce decisions on nonmonetary incentives,[b] such as siting of unrelated federal facilities (for purposes of economic development and employment generation), and on provision of federal grants for programs related to storage and disposal siting (such as development of emergency response capabilities)	Yes(B)*	Yes(B)	Yes(I)

Table 4.3—Continued

Critical Organizational Attribute	Structural and Procedural Feature	Can the Model Have the Feature?		
		PRIVCORP	GOVCORP	IGA
Technical capabilities to conduct the scientific and engineering research, analysis, design, and demonstration and the environmental regulation compliance activities required for the license application process, and to manage and evaluate such work undertaken by contractors *and* Technical capabilities to make science-based decisions that meet the highest standards for safety and human health and environmental protection *and* Technical capabilities to undertake site evaluation, selection, and planning	Exemptions from federal personnel rules, to provide flexibility in hiring and firing and in attracting talented technical experts; for GOVCORP and agency, exemptions could be limited to certain classes of employees with specified skills and experience	Yes(I)	Yes(B)	Yes(B)
Management capabilities to plan and implement megaprojects, either directly or through oversight and evaluation of contractors	Exemptions from federal personnel rules, to provide flexibility in hiring and firing and in attracting talented managers	Yes(I)	Yes(B)[c]	Yes(B)
	Exemptions from federal contracting requirements, to provide flexibility in procurement	Yes(I)	Yes(B)[c]	Yes(B)
	Access to capital for construction of facilities	Yes(B)	Yes(B)	Yes(B)
Legal capacity to procure services; purchase, lease, and dispose of land and other property; and hold title to spent fuel	Necessary legal capacities written into enabling legislation/charter	Yes(B)	Yes(B)	Yes(B)
	Exemptions from federal contracting requirements, to provide flexibility in procurement	Yes(I)	Yes(B)[c]	Yes(B)

[a] This feature would be applicable for a board or commission of an IGA but not for a single administrator model. With respect to PRIVCORPs and GOVCORPs, *governance board* refers to a board of directors.

[b] Regarding the importance of nonmonetary incentives, see Stewart, 2008, pp. 823–824.

[c] See Chapter Three for a discussion of how federal personnel and procurement rules apply to GOVCORPs.

NOTES:

YES(I) = the attribute the feature is meant to produce is inherent to the model

YES(B) = it is possible to build the feature into the model, generally through congressional mandate (enabling legislation or charter).

YES(B)* = it is theoretically possible, but not typical, for Congress to build the feature into the model, and we are not aware of precedent.

NO = the feature is incompatible with the model.

"Not needed" indicates that the feature is not needed because the problem the feature is meant to address is not present in the organizational form.

a role for the President in the appointment of the MDO leader and governance bodies (the precise nature of the leader and any governance body varies in accordance with the model, as explained in Chapter Three) and a role for the Senate in their confirmation. Under the GOVCORP model, the MDO leader (chief executive) would not typically be a presidential appointee, but that feature is not impossible. Under the PRIVCORP model, presidential appointment of the board of directors would be conceptually inconsistent with the private, for-profit nature of the enterprise, which implies shareholder oversight (in principle) of the board and typically involves board self-selection.

Congressional oversight would be typical for an IGA and could be exercised for a GOVCORP (and details could be written into the charter), but it would not typically be exercised with respect to a PRIVCORP and would be inconsistent with the arms-length nature of the model, though Congress always could resort to using its subpoena power.

Devising means for accountability to state and tribal authorities could be important for gaining the consent of these authorities to siting, as illustrated by the WIPP experience in New Mexico. Under any of the three models, the enabling legislation or charter could specify that the states and tribal authorities with jurisdiction over areas in which facilities are sited could have a regulatory role, for the protection of human health and the environment, alongside that of federal regulatory bodies. State or tribal responsibility for implementation and enforcement of environmental statutes is already in place, for example, under the federal Clean Air Act, Clean Water Act, and the Resource Conservation and Recovery Act.[12]

An additional feature feasible for the IGA and GOVCORP models would be creation of an independent IG, with public reporting responsibilities. This degree of ongoing and focused government oversight would be conceptually inconsistent with the PRIVCORP model, which is based on the notion of oversight by shareholders and a board of directors.

Transparent Decisionmaking

Developing an organizational culture that embraces transparency may be the MDO's most important means of ensuring that its decisionmaking processes are open and transparent. The MDO's leadership will have principal responsibility for inculcating that culture—organizational features can provide only partial and limited means. That said, such features as notification and participation requirements and public-meeting requirements written into the enabling legislation or charter could be helpful. These could be built into any of the three basic models or variations within the models, though it would be conceptually inconsistent with a PRIVCORP to dictate such procedures to it.[13]

---

[12] 42 U.S.C., ch. 85; 33 U.S.C. § 1251 et seq.; 42 U.S.C. § 6901 et seq.

[13] Private corporations can take the initiative to subject themselves to increased public scrutiny, but a congressional mandate for such oversight would be unprecedented.

Creating an independent IG with public reporting responsibilities, discussed earlier with respect to accountability, could also foster at least post hoc transparency of the MDO's decisions and operations. This option would be consistent with the IGA or GOVCORP model but not the PRIVCORP model.

Political Credibility and Influence

Political credibility and influence are intangible attributes and will depend to a significant extent on the personal characteristics of the MDO's leadership and the organization's ability to gain political backing for its negotiating approaches and decisions. Certain organizational design features may, however, give the MDO the capability of developing such backing and may help create the perception on the part of states, tribes, and local communities that the MDO will be able to deliver results if they engage with it in a negotiating process.

Political connections with the President, Congress, and states and tribes will be important. How the leadership of the MDO is structured and selected, and the relationships of individual leaders to stakeholder groups and political authorities, will have significant effects on the organization's credibility and influence. Presidential nomination and Senate confirmation for appointment of leaders would help build connectedness to those authorities. If a decision is made that the MDO will be an IGA, then a multimember board or commission variation of that model would typically provide more connectedness to Congress and, through it, local interests than would a single administrator reporting to the President.[14]

For the MDO to have negotiating leverage in the siting process, it will also be crucial for it to be able to deliver the consensus of the whole federal government.[15] A direct role in the executive branch interagency process, as would be the case for an IGA, would be one way. This approach would be enhanced if the MDO were statutorily designated as having the lead role in developing consensus and cooperation among agencies having regulatory roles in siting, transportation, and related matters. Another way could be to set up, under the Domestic Policy Council, OMB or Secretary of Energy, an ad hoc interagency group with representation from the executive departments, the regulatory agencies, and the MDO leadership.[16]

Gaining the support of stakeholder interests can help the MDO build political credibility and influence as well. The creation of a governance board or advisory board whose members are aligned with stakeholder interests, including the interests of states,

---

[14] See Stewart, 2008, pp. 813–814.

[15] See Stewart, 2008, p. 799, regarding Bureau of Indian Affairs and Bureau of Land Management blockage of Private Fuel Storage consortium facility in Utah after NRC granted a license in 2006.

[16] The executive branch has used this approach in connection with the San Francisco Bay–San Joaquin–Sacramento Delta debate in California, in which four federal agencies had separate and conflicting regulatory requirements; the Florida Everglades; and most recently the Gulf States Task Force following the *Deepwater Horizon* (BP) oil spill.

tribes, and local communities as well as the utilities, could be a useful means of gaining support. The composition of such boards could be mandated under the GOVCORP or IGA models; a PRIVCORP would typically have discretion to make such decisions, and mandates in this regard would be conceptually inconsistent with the model, though not impossible.[17]

Insulation from Political Control

Though Congress has wide latitude in how it structures the charter for a PRIVCORP or a GOVCORP, as discussed in Chapter Three, under the basic concepts of these models, the former is inherently insulated from political control and the latter is largely insulated. As an entity normally subject to political control, however, an IGA would need special features to achieve such insulation.

The multimember board or commission model of governance is a variation that Congress has employed when, among other rationales, it wishes to invest an IGA with considerable autonomy. This approach can be used to ensure ideological balance in the governance body and the representation of a variety of interests and to limit presidential control, which, in principle, is greater under a single-administrator model of governance.[18] For an IGA administrator or chairperson of a multimember board or commission, a fixed, lengthy term of office and a term limit could minimize that individual's susceptibility to political pressure and, by creating overlap between the term and different administrations, could, at least in principle, encourage the administrator or chairperson to take a longer-term view of MDO decisions than would otherwise be the case. Similarly, limiting the grounds for removal of the MDO administrator or chairperson to for-cause removal, with the applicable causes specified, would protect the person holding that position from pressure to weigh short-term political considerations heavily in decisionmaking.

Another way under any of the organizational models to achieve insulation from political control is to limit review of siting decisions to judicial authorities (i.e., no review by the President or by other executive branch authorities, except in the context of their exercise of specified regulatory functions). This feature would be inherent in a PRIVCORP and GOVCORP and could be built into an IGA. Under any model, judicial authorities would be able to review MDO decisions to the extent of their jurisdiction.

---

[17] Such boards exist in both the private and public sectors. For example, private companies managing large-scale facilities often establish community action panels that include representatives of the surrounding community (e.g., environmental groups, local officials, community organizations) to advise and provide feedback. The Federal Reserve serves as a public-sector example, with its consumer advisory council that is made up of members who represent consumers, communities, and creditors. The council meets with the board of governors three times per year and advises on consumer financial services. See Board of Governors of the Federal Reserve System, 2005.

[18] Regarding congressional rationales for creating independent agencies, see Devins and Lewis, 2008. The authors point out that independence in principle does not always translate into independence in practice.

Insulation from congressional pressure can best be assured through implementation of a funding model that does not require the MDO to be dependent on annual appropriations because the appropriations process is Congress's greatest vehicle for exerting its influence. In principle, this is possible under any of the three models.

Organizational Stability: Durability

The MDO's durability cannot be guaranteed through its organizational design, regardless of which model is selected.[19] Though the federal government as a whole may be more durable than any non- or quasi-governmental enterprise, particular federal agencies are no more inherently durable than such enterprises.

Dynamics that could threaten the MDO's durability could be mitigated, however. Most important will be ensuring that the MDO's financial solvency can be assured to the extent possible. Ensuring that it is not dependent on annual appropriations would be one means applicable to all three models, though the unavailability of appropriations could leave the organization financially vulnerable if other funding streams are not reliable. U.S. government backing of the MDO's debt would be another means, though this would not be typical for a PRIVCORP or GOVCORP.

The MDO's ability to adapt to its changing functional requirements over time will be an important element of ensuring its durability. The MDO will have responsibility for multiple phases of development of storage and disposal solutions and a multiplicity of functions within each phase. The initial phase—siting of storage and disposal facilities—entails significantly different organizational requirements than the later stages. In particular, siting will require the MDO to manage a politically sensitive process of eliciting the consent of states, tribes, and local communities. Construction of facilities once sited, however, will require management of major infrastructure development projects. Thus, the MDO will need to be able to adapt its processes, personnel, and possibly its structure over time as the functional emphasis of its work shifts from siting to construction to management and operation of facilities. In instances in which another organization is the licensee, the MDO will have to maintain an oversight role to ensure that the organization conducts its activities consistent with national interests and consent-based processes.

The PRIVCORP and GOVCORP models, at least in principle, are inherently capable of adapting to changing missions and business need. IGAs may be less adaptable, though it is possible to build in features that would enable it to change its pro-

---

[19]   See Boin, Kuipers, and Steenbergen, 2010, which finds that no combination of design options for a government agency will guarantee its organizational survival and that it is more effective to design for adaptation than for survival. These researchers and others have, however, identified some design characteristics of public institutions that tend to help them endure over time. These include insulation from the President, putting the organization outside an executive office or cabinet structure, establishment through law, and having a board or commission structure rather than a single administrator. See Lewis, 2003; and Boin, Kuipers, and Steenbergen, 2010, pp. 385–410.

cesses as its responsibilities change. In particular, options could be considered for ways of ensuring that the MDO employs a different decisionmaking approach to siting, which has a crucial consensus-building element, than to construction and other functions that will follow siting over time. One way in which Congress has affected government agency decisionmaking processes in the past when consideration of a variety of interests is especially important is by requiring the establishment of a study group.[20] The study group's conclusions could be advisory, or the agency could be required to reflect them in its decisions. In conjunction with establishing the MDO, a study group representing a range of stakeholder interests could be formed solely for the siting phase. This approach could offer some of the benefits of assigning the siting role to a multimember commission without the detriment of having to create a new, more suitable organizational form when siting is completed and construction and operation of facilities become the focus of the MDO's work.

Organizational Stability: Policy Consistency

The need to ensure consistency of policy direction applies principally to the IGA model, which can be vulnerable to policy shifts that reflect changing political preferences. Thus, under this model, features are needed that mitigate the incentives to shift policy. Features that constrain the politicization of the appointment and removal of MDO leaders are especially useful in this regard. These include imposing a limit on the number or percentage of political appointees in the organization; setting fixed and staggered terms, and requiring political party–affiliation balance, for members of a multimember board or commission; and setting a fixed, lengthy term for an MDO single administrator or chairperson of a board or commission. Under any of the three models (though not typically for a PRIVCORP), substantive qualifications for the MDO leader could be specified in the enabling legislation or charter. This feature would imply, but not require, that the leader (an administrator, chairperson, or chief executive) should be a person with relevant expertise rather than a political figure.

Although the PRIVCORP and GOVCORP models do not have the same vulnerability to political wind-shifting as the IGA model, this does not mean that guarantees of consistency are inherent to the two models. Consistency relies principally on the behavior of the board of directors. Under both models, the chief executive is accountable to the board of directors, which, in principle, provides oversight and ensures stability. In the case of a PRIVCORP, the board watches to make sure that profit is made; for a GOVCORP, the board watches to ensure that the defined mission is being carried out. In both cases, the measures analogous to those that would insulate an agency head from political control would be inappropriate because the chief executive's discretion would not be adequately checked.

---

[20] See McCubbins, Noll, and Weingast, 1989, pp. 474–479.

It is important to note that there may be trade-offs between policy consistency and flexibility—both of which are important organizational attributes.[21] If policy stability is important, then statutory constraints on flexibility will be more effective than oversight. Flexibility can be constrained by writing into the enabling legislation or charter precisely what the MDO is to achieve and how. But the uncertainty of technical knowledge and the need for a consent-based process imply that policy outcomes for the MDO cannot be specified in detail at the outset; experience with the overly rigid provisions of the NWPA demonstrate the potential adverse consequences of a constraining approach.

Organizational Stability: Management

Management stability will be important for the PRIVCORP and GOVCORP models, but, as with policy consistency, will likely depend on the conduct of the board of directors. Staggered terms for board members are common in the business world but for continuity reasons, not to ensure political balance as with a multimember board or commission variation of an IGA. For a PRIVCORP in particular, constraining shareholder and board control of management through any features intended to ensure management stability would erode the essential nature of the private enterprise.

Under the IGA model, management consistency can be fostered—though not guaranteed—through many of the same features discussed with respect to policy consistency and other attributes: fixed and staggered terms for members of a multimember board or commission; a fixed, lengthy term and term limit for an MDO administrator or chairperson; limited grounds for removal of the administrator or chairperson; and a limit on the number or percentage of political appointees (whose service is typically of short duration). All of these features would tend to reduce management turnover.

Clear Mandate to Decide on Siting

Ensuring that the MDO has a clear mandate to be the authority responsible for siting decisions (subject to licensing and regulatory procedures) and the associated legal capacity will be a matter of writing such language into the enabling legislation or charter. This could be done for any of the three models, though it should be noted that this would likely be most difficult for the PRIVCORP model because the mandate would mean that what had been a governmental function was being handed over to a commercial, for-profit enterprise. Less tangibly, under any of the three models, high-level policy direction will be needed to ensure that federal regulatory agencies and the Executive Office of the President will treat the MDO as being the responsible entity and will demonstrate cooperation with it and support execution of mission.

---

[21]   Regarding this trade-off, see McCubbins, Noll, and Weingast, 1989, p. 440.

Ability to Commit to Incentives

The ability to commit to provide incentives (including economic development incentives) for potential sites requires control over resources to fund incentives and the discretion to allocate those resources. The MDO's discretion will need to be subject to auditing for financial accountability and judicial review for compliance with the MDO's enabling legislation or charter. This attribute would be facilitated by the MDO not being subject to review of the merits of allocation decisions, so that agreements it makes will have finality. The MDO's enabling legislation or charter could give it final authority to use its resources to fund incentives.

For nonmonetary incentives, direct involvement in the executive branch interagency process (possible only under the IGA model) would best enable the MDO to influence decisions, such as siting of unrelated federal facilities in communities that host waste storage or disposal facilities, and agreement to and implementation of federal programs related to storage and disposal siting, such as development of state and local emergency response capabilities. An alternative would be to set up interagency processes with representation from the MDO leadership.

Technical Capabilities

For the MDO to have the many important technical capabilities it needs, the key will be for it to attract and retain personnel having the requisite technical expertise. A PRIVCORP and, typically (given how their charters are usually written), a GOVCORP will be able to compete freely in the labor marketplace for such experts, though they will need to be assured of financial resources for attracting the necessary talent. An IGA will be subject to federal personnel rules that will constrain the MDO's ability to compete in this respect, unless statutory exemptions are provided. Exemptions could be limited to certain categories or a certain number of employees. Such exemptions are feasible but may be politically difficult to secure. It should be noted at the same time that civil service protections could be attractive to at least some classes of employees that the MDO will need to hire and that federal personnel rules exist to provide transparency and legitimacy. However, given the phased nature of the MDO's responsibilities, it is important to consider that termination restrictions could impinge on the MDO's ability to adapt to its changing functional emphasis over time.

Capabilities to Manage Megaprojects

The megaprojects that the MDO will be responsible for implementing will place extraordinary management demands on the organization—beyond ordinary project management requirements. The facilities that the MDO must establish will have to meet exceptional technical and safety standards and, for repositories in particular, will present unprecedented construction challenges. Much of the work for which the MDO will be responsible is likely to be undertaken by contractors regardless of the model adopted, but the MDO will need a talented and sufficiently sized cadre of managers to oversee major contracts. The points made in the previous section regarding attracting and retaining technical personnel are equally applicable with respect to management personnel.

The MDO also may need contracting flexibility in order to undertake the major projects required. A PRIVCORP will inherently have such flexibility; a GOVCORP normally will as well, though specific exemptions from federal contracting rules may need to be written into its charter, depending on whether the GOVCORP is wholly or partially government owned. An IGA could need exemptions from federal contracting requirements. As with personnel requirements, such exemptions are feasible but may be politically difficult to secure.

Under all three models, the MDO will need access to capital in order to implement megaprojects. All three afford the means for accessing capital but in different ways. A PRIVCORP would rely on capital markets; an IGA would secure capital from the U.S. Treasury; and a GOVCORP could rely on a combination of both, depending on the specific terms of its charter.

Legal Capacity to Procure Services and Property

The legal capacities the MDO will need—to procure services; purchase, lease, and dispose of land and other property; and hold title to spent fuel—should not prove difficult to write into the enabling legislation or charter under any of the three models. Cost-effective procurement could require some exemptions from federal contracting rules, however. As noted in the previous section, federal contracting rules would apply to an IGA and some types of GOVCORPs, unless exemptions are provided. Such exemptions are feasible but could be politically difficult to obtain.

Discriminating Among Organizational Models

Our analysis shows that many of the structural and procedural features needed to produce the critical organizational attributes are present or can be built into the three organizational models. The "No" entries in Table 4.3, which indicate that the feature is incompatible with the model, are limited in number.

Nevertheless, several critical attributes are weaker or missing from the PRIVCORP model. For the critical attribute of political credibility and influence needed for the siting process, three features relating to linkages to the executive branch are conceptually inconsistent with the PRIVCORP model. Though these features could theoretically be written into a PRIVCORP's charter, doing so would distort the organization's private-enterprise character. Public trust could be weaker under the PRIVCORP model than in the other two models because of lack of congressional oversight and incompatibility with a mandated IG feature. Perhaps most significant is that creating an organization with a public interest mission would be inconsistent with a for-profit PRIVCORP.[22] (Indeed, removing Congress and the executive branch from decisionmaking is a key motivation for establishing a PRIVCORP.) Putting the public's interests above any private interests will be essential to achieving the performance goal of ensuring that the MDO's decisions and actions meet the highest standards for long-term public safety and protection of human health and the environment.

Distinctions exist as well between the two other organizational models. Some features are typical of an IGA but not a GOVCORP: direct participation in the executive branch interagency process and direct influence in decisions regarding nonmonetary incentives for siting that the federal government could provide. Features that are inherent to the GOVCORP model (and the PRIVCORP model) that would have to be built into an IGA model include insulation from political control and management and operational flexibility. All of these distinctions point to trade-offs between the IGA and GOVCORP models but not superiority of one model over another.

---

[22] In Sweden, the Nuclear Fuel and Waste Management Company (SNF), a private corporation formed by nuclear power plant owners, is responsible for waste management; some of these nuclear plants are partly government-owned. In our view, the public confidence and trust built up by the Swedish utilities within a relatively homogenous society is not something that could be replicated in as large and diverse a country as the United States. Further, Sweden does not have the equivalent of state-level governments as in the United States. Finally, both these countries are dealing with a single waste form (used fuel), not the complex inventory that the United States has of used and defense high-level waste. Together, these factors suggest that the Swedish model is unlikely to be a viable option in the United States.

CHAPTER FIVE

Designing a New Management and Disposition Organization

Presidents and Congress have considerable flexibility in designing organizations seeking to balance the advantages of a government entity (longevity, political influence, and public accountability) with the advantages of a private corporation (independence and internal flexibility). Indeed, policymakers have flexibility in choosing not only among the three organizational models (IGA, GOVCORP, and PRIVCORP) but also the specific characteristics within each of the models.

Although there could be reasons for picking one organizational model over another on the basis of their characteristics, we discovered that more analysis was required with a focus on the critical attributes an organization needs to achieve its performance goals and carry out its responsibilities. In the case of an MDO, these critical attributes include, for example, political credibility and influence to accomplish consent-based siting of the facilities; accountability; transparent decisionmaking; ability to commit to providing incentives; insulation from political control; a public interest mission; and organizational stability (durability and consistency in policy and management).

From our analysis matching the critical attributes with the organizational models, we came to the view that several critical attributes are weaker in or missing from the PRIVCORP model, including public accountability, public interest mission, and linkages to the executive branch and Congress that would ensure the political credibility and influence needed for siting. Although these features could theoretically be written into a PRIVCORP's charter, achieving these would be prohibitively difficult for a U.S. private corporation whose primary loyalty is to its stockholders in earning a profit.

These critical attributes, however, exist or can be built into the two other organizational models—an IGA and a GOVCORP—given the many different variations in the characteristics that these organizations can take. At the same time, the organizational models do differ in the emphasis given to different attributes, and these differences provide a point of departure for policymakers to design a new MDO.

Policymakers' Choices

In designing a new MDO, policymakers will need to go through a series of steps that will involve a number of choices, first about the relationship of the MDO to the President, next about Congress's role, third about the source of the MDO's funding, and then the role of stakeholders and other MDO organizational features. We begin with the President and Congress because their roles are critical in setting the tone and shaping the relationship among the MDO, stakeholders, and the public.

Step 1: The President's Role

The critical choice for policymakers is how the MDO should relate to the President, i.e., whether it should be a direct relationship, as in an IGA, or a relationship that is largely independent of the President, as in a GOVCORP. See Figure 5.1.

- **Direct relationship:** Reporting directly to the President, as with an IGA, ensures that the public interest is taken into account in all the operations of the MDO. The influence residing with the President would be available to achieve the siting of the storage and disposal facilities, and the executive branch would be able to influence MDO operations in ways to make certain that the siting tasks are being

Figure 5.1
The MDO's Relationship to the President

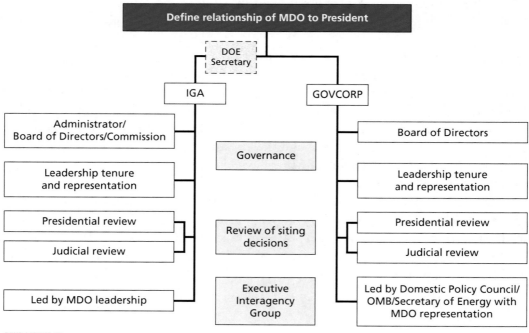

accomplished; the storage, transport, and disposal of used fuel and nuclear waste are being carried out safely; and situations do not arise in which a government bailout would be needed.

- **Independent relationship:** Greater independence from the President, as is typically the case in a GOVCORP, insulates the activities of the MDO from the turnover of administrations, provides the authority necessary to make decisions on siting without political interference, and allows flexibility in siting negotiations, operations (including contracting and procurement), and personnel policy.

Ultimately, the choice of an IGA or GOVCORP turns on how to strike the balance between competing values: ensuring the public interest, influence on MDO operations, and political credibility versus providing political autonomy and insulation as well as flexibility in the conduct of the MDO activities.

In the case of an IGA, policymakers would have the choice of whether the MDO would report to the President directly or through the Secretary of Energy, as is the case today with BPA. This would be different from the past when OCRWM was an office inside DOE. Reporting through the Secretary of Energy would be a way for MDO activities to continue to be closely integrated with other DOE-related activities, e.g., operating the facilities at Savannah River, South Carolina; Rocky Flats, Colorado; National Laboratory, Idaho; and the Hanford Reservation, Washington State and managing research and other activities related to the development of new reactor and fuel cycle technologies. The case for having the MDO report directly to the President rests largely on the need to make a break from past problems associated with DOE's management of used fuel and defense high-level nuclear waste, particularly the Yucca Mountain program, and the loss of public trust and confidence that resulted.

Having chosen either an IGA or a GOVCORP, policymakers will have some flexibility to build into the organization features to enhance its prospects of achieving its performance goals and lessen some of the potential disadvantages associated with the organizational form chosen. This would be accomplished through the enabling legislation. Policymakers would have choices in three areas: governance, presidential review of MDO decisions, and the interagency process needed to facilitate cooperation among the executive agencies.

Independent Government Agency

If an IGA is preferred, policymakers would first need to choose its supervisory structure, i.e., whether the agency would be led by a governing board (e.g., the Federal Reserve), a commission (e.g., NRC), or a single administrator (e.g., BPA, NASA). While maintaining public accountability, steps could then be taken to shape the governance of an IGA to achieve some degree of political insulation. A balance among political affiliations could be mandated for a multimember board or commission, as well as representation of a variety of stakeholder interests. The members could also be given fixed and staggered terms extending beyond four years. In the case of a single administrator, the term could be extended beyond that of a four-year presidential administration. The grounds for removal of these officials could also be limited, e.g., for-cause removal, with causes specified. These officials would still be nominated by the President and there will be the need to find ways to expedite the process so as not to leave the MDO without the leadership that it will need.

To further build political insulation and organizational stability, policymakers could preclude presidential review of the MDO's major decisions, including siting, and limit review of siting decisions to judicial authorities (i.e., no review by the President or by other executive branch agencies, except in the context of their exercise of specified regulatory functions).

The IGA administrator or board/commission chairman could also be designated to lead an interagency group to ensure the political credibility and influence necessary to carry out the MDO's responsibilities, particularly in siting when incentives will need to be found and in licensing when approval will be required from many different regulatory agencies with missions that may not coincide with the MDO's.

Government Corporation

To increase the accountability of the leadership in a GOVCORP, policymakers could require in the legislative charter that the President nominate the members of the MDO's board of directors and mandate that their terms be relatively short and subject to periodic renewal. As with an IGA, there will be the need to find ways to expedite the process so as not to leave the MDO without the leadership that it will need. In addition to defining what experience and expertise they wished to have on the board, policymakers could designate a member of the executive branch to serve *ex-officio* on the board. As a GOVCORP is designed to be insulated from presidential involvement, policymakers could make provision for some presidential role and review of the MDO's major decisions.

To tap into the resources of the federal government for providing the incentives that will be necessary to achieve the siting of the facilities and to gain influence over the activities of the executive branch agencies, including the regulators, policymakers could set up, under the Domestic Policy Council, OMB, or the Secretary of Energy, an ad hoc group with representation from the executive departments, the regulatory agencies, and the GOVCORP leadership.

Step 2: Congress's Role

Policymakers will also need to address the relationship of the MDO to Congress and focus on oversight and the congressional role in decisions on siting. These will be independent of which organizational model is chosen. See Figure 5.2.

Policymakers will need to decide whether the Senate will have a role in confirming the leadership of the MDO: the board of directors, commission, or agency admin-

Figure 5.2
The MDO's Relationship to the Congress and Funding Source

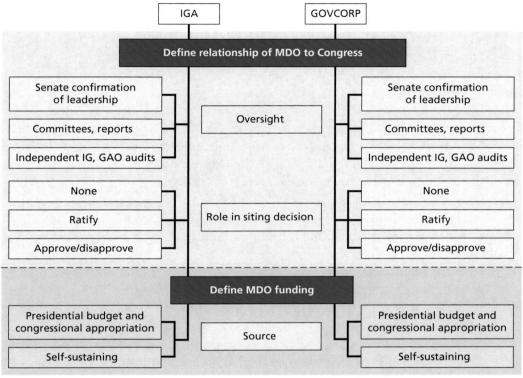

RAND *MG1230-5.2*

istrator. If there is a role in confirmation, the Senate will need to put in place processes to avoid delays that could leave the MDO without the leadership it needs.

Policymakers will also need to make decisions as to which committees will exercise oversight over the operations and decisions of the MDO and through what types of testimonies and reports (on, for example, strategic plans, management and financial operations). To gain insight into the conduct of MDO activities, Congress could create an independent IG who is required to submit annual public reports and require audits by the GAO.

Finally, policymakers will need to decide whether Congress will be given any specific role in the various decisions that will be called for in the siting processes, i.e., the locations of the facilities and the agreements negotiated with states, tribes, and local communities. One possibility is for Congress to ratify these MDO decisions (e.g., as the Senate ratifies a treaty in an "up-down" vote); another possibility is that Congress approve or disapprove these decisions (e.g., as is done with the recommendations of the Base Closing and Realignment Commission to close military facilities).

History has shown that, under the terms and conditions of the NWPA, Congress fully involved itself in site selection, funding, and regulatory decisions and, in so doing, undermined public trust and confidence in the processes. Although Congress does have an important and constructive role to play in the future, there is an inherent tension between a consent-based siting approach and giving Congress the authority to veto agreements made between the MDO and consenting states, tribes, and local communities.

Step 3: MDO Funding

Perhaps the most important issue that policymakers face is what will be the source of the MDO's funding, i.e., whether it will receive annual congressional appropriations or be able to fund its expenditures from operating revenues or other resources (i.e., "self-sustaining"). See Figure 5.2. The decision on how the MDO is funded is independent of whether the organization is a GOVCORP or an IGA. TVA (a GOVCORP) has a dedicated funding stream; the NRC (an IGA) has a dedicated funding stream but is subject to an annual appropriation, and Amtrak (a GOVCORP) has both dedicated funding streams and annual appropriations. NASA (an IGA) receives annual appropriations.

In the case of annual appropriations, the Senate and House will be required to authorize and appropriate the funds, and the MDO will need to submit its budget through OMB and provide the supporting budget justification and documentation to the various congressional oversight committees. Even if funds are made available on a self-sustaining basis through a dedicated funding source, OMB and the Congress could still exercise oversight by requiring the MDO to submit quarterly and annual financial and management reports.

Step 4: Other Organizational Features

Whether an IGA or GOVCORP model is chosen, policymakers will need to define other features of a new MDO and include these in the enabling legislation: one is how the MDO will relate to its stakeholders, another is how it will be treated by federal and state regulatory agencies, a third is what responsibilities it will have for the management and disposition of both commercial and defense materials, and finally whether the MDO will be subject to federal personnel, procurement, and contracting rules. See Figure 5.3.

Relationship to Stakeholders

The MDO will have multiple stakeholders (utility companies, states, local communities, tribes, NGOs, as well as the U.S. Department of Defense [DoD] and DOE), so policymakers will need to decide how these interests will be represented within the MDO itself or through different coordination and consultation mechanisms. One way is to call for their representation on a board of directors or commission and write into

Figure 5.3
Other Organizational Features of the MDO

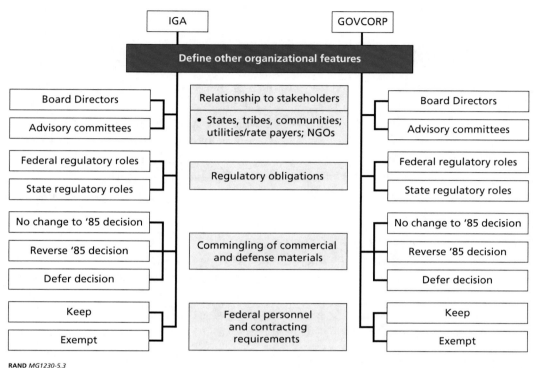

the enabling legislation specific requirements in terms of the different stakeholders. Another way is to set up advisory committees to gain advice and support with participation by some or all of these stakeholders. For example, an Advisory Siting Council could be established to provide oversight of the siting process, with representation from states, tribes, local communities, environmental groups, the utilities, and rate payers.[1] Still another way, a variation on TVA's approach in the 1930s, is to encourage a very aggressive operational outreach that puts officials on the ground and in direct contact with the people and communities, simultaneously focused on education and persuasion, but also on listening with humility.

Regulatory Obligations and Liabilities

Although there are some theoretical differences in how federal agencies and private corporations are treated in terms of their regulatory obligations, the responsibilities of the MDO will likely call for similar treatment from the NRC, EPA, and other federal regulatory agencies. In fact, it is not clear that there are major choices for policymak-

---

[1]   AMFM, 1984, pp. X-2, XI-6.

ers to make about federal environmental health and safety regulations, but there *is* a choice to be made regarding the regulatory role of states with respect to the sited facilities for protection of human health and the environment. A prominent role for state regulators was critical to the ultimate success in siting the WIPP facility in Carlsbad, New Mexico.

Policymakers will also need to address the liability issues associated with the MDO's assumption of title to used fuel and nuclear waste, given the risks and costs tied to these materials. However the liability regime is shaped, the MDO will need Congress to confer authority to take title and articulate the specific conditions under which the MDO is expected to do so (i.e., what the MDO will be expected to get from the utilities in return). The most critical point here is to ensure that the mistake of NWPA is not repeated by tying transfer of title to a specific date rather than a specific performance milestone. No organization will be able to control the precise timing of the siting process, given the unpredictability of reaching agreement with affected states, tribes, and local communities.

Commingling of Commercial and Defense Materials

Policymakers will need to decide whether the MDO will be responsible for the management and disposition of both commercial and defense materials. An analysis of the choices (maintain the 1985 decision of commingled repository, reverse the 1985 decision and separate the repositories, or defer the decision) was outside the scope of this study but is being addressed by DOE in its analyses of the BRC recommendations.[2] Whatever the choice, there will be implications for the design of the MDO, because funding for commercial and defense materials will come from different sources: i.e., the costs of commercial used fuel would come from revenues from nuclear utility ratepayers; defense and other government-owned used fuel and high-level waste would be funded through DOD and DOE appropriations. If a decision is made to continue a policy of commingling, organizational processes will be needed to manage the two funding streams in a unified manner, and this could be done for either an IGA or GOVCORP. Liability and ownership of defense high-level nuclear waste within a GOVCORP framework would require specific legislative language but could be accomplished. More challenging perhaps would be the capability and agility of the GOVCORP model to respond to unforeseen and potentially large national security needs.

Federal Personnel, Procurement, and Contracting

An IGA would typically be bound by federal personnel rules and federal procurement and contracting requirements. To be able to attract the technical expertise and management talent as well as gain flexibility in hiring and firing, policymakers could

---

[2]   For the 1985 decision, see Ronald Reagan, letter to Secretary of Energy John S. Herrington, "Disposal of Defense Waste in a Commercial Repository," Washington, D.C., April 30, 1985.

exempt the new MDO from the personnel rules for some or all classes of employees. To provide flexibility for managing multiyear megaprojects, policymakers could provide flexibility to enable funding obligations for multi-year contracts, or could exempt the IGA from the federal procurement and contracting requirements.

Given that the rationale for forming a GOVCORP typically involves allowing the organization "to run on business-like principles," these entities are often exempted from at least some aspects of federal personnel management, procurement, and contracting requirements.

Whether formed as an IGA or GOVCORP, policymakers will need to decide in its enabling legislation whether to exempt the MDO from these requirements (see Chapter Three).

Amending the Enabling Legislation

Congress will always have the authority to amend the legislation that establishes the MDO. Policymakers will need to decide whether they wish to introduce in the enabling legislation for a new MDO any requirements for how this might be done, e.g., by requiring a simple or super majority vote.

Considerations Related to Choice of Organizational Form

Government Responsibility for Catastrophic Risk

In making a decision on the organizational form of a new MDO, policymakers will need to consider what role the U.S. government would play in situations in which major financial problems or other serious dangers arise. In an IGA, there would be no question that the government would have ultimate responsibility for any future risks (or catastrophic liability) that might arise in connection with managing used fuel and high-level waste. In contrast, a GOVCORP would not be backed by the full faith and credit of the U.S. government (unless Congress decided to make it so), and, at least in principle, the government would not necessarily be obligated to step in and bail out a GOVCORP. [3] Nevertheless, given the nature of the mission of managing used fuel, and the inherent and long-term risks that attach to this task, it is difficult to imagine

---

[3]   Depending on exactly how Congress chooses to structure a GOVCORP to serve as an MDO, it is entirely possible that the terms of the Price-Anderson Act of 1957 (codified 42 USC § 2210) could apply. The Price-Anderson Act involves a set of provisions for insuring the operation of commercial nuclear power plants in the United States, together with a set of related DOE contractor activities, against potentially catastrophic incidents. Without getting deeply into the details, the Price-Anderson Act provides a mechanism to partly insure related risks; to cap the liability faced by commercial participants in the nuclear power industry; and to obligate Congress to revisit liability compensation above the cap, in the event of a highly consequential nuclear incident. To the extent that the Price-Anderson Act does apply to a future MDO (structured in the form of GOVCORP), that means first that some fraction of catastrophic liability risk would need to be insured pursuant to the terms of the Act; and second, in the event of a catastrophe, Congress would then be on the hook to consider and execute plans for additional compensation, to the extent needed.

that a difference would exist in practice: If a catastrophic risk event affecting large numbers of people and the environment were to occur, the U.S. government would be placed under tremendous pressure to take responsibility and to intervene to manage the risk.[4]

Evolution of the MDO as Its Roles Change Over Time

Given the varied responsibilities of the MDO and the time to accomplish its multiple tasks, policymakers will also need to consider whether an MDO should be created as a single fixed organization to carry out all its responsibilities over a long period of time or whether the MDO should be designed with characteristics that would change to meet the demands of different phases of its mission.

The argument for a fixed organization is that anticipated evolution of its organizational design could undermine the ability of the MDO to develop its own culture and management skills for carrying out its highly complex and multifaceted activities over the long term. Moreover, many of the MDO activities will need to be pursued simultaneously. On the other hand, the organizational culture and skills for achieving the siting of the consolidated storage and permanent disposal sites through a consent-based process will be very different from those required to successfully pursue a license application, construct multiple facilities, and then operate and close those facilities. When the organization is predominantly in its siting phase, it will require a skilled staff of negotiators, technical advisors, risk communicators, and individuals adept at public outreach. When the organization is predominantly in the phases of preparing a license application and planning construction, it will require individuals with sophisticated technical and project management skills teamed with strong public communicators.

One approach would be to choose a GOVCORP because of its inherent flexibility to hire and fire people easily, to change its own internal structure, and make decisions about when and how to contract out various tasks and functions. Another approach is to design the MDO to evolve by design, starting with an IGA, which embodies what will be needed to achieve consent-based siting: a close relationship to the President, public accountability, access to the resources of the federal government, and the ability to enter into long-term agreements. Depending on how they are led and managed, either a GOVCORP or IGA has the potential to achieve public trust.

Under either an IGA or GOVCORP, Congress could include a provision in the enabling legislation for periodic evaluations of organizational effectiveness, which could then provide the analytical basis for determining whether refinements or structural changes are warranted in the future. This is something akin to an adaptive management approach, embedded in the program now operating in Canada and Sweden,

---

[4]   See the response of the U.S. government to the BP oil spill (National Commission on the BP Deepwater Horizon Oil Spill and Offshore Drilling, 2011).

among others.[5] If the view is that the MDO may need to evolve in its organizational design, policymakers would need to address this in the enabling legislation. A transition could be provided within the structure of the enabling organization, or new legislation could be mandated.

Making the Choices

The success of any future MDO will be driven by many factors and unforeseen circumstances. The organizational form is only one of these factors: it is a necessary but not sufficient condition for success. Beyond the organization itself, the evolution of national priorities and changes in the political environment will have a profound effect on the success of any MDO in meeting the performance goals articulated by the BRC and outlined here. There is almost certainly more than one way to design a successful MDO. Still, it is likely the case that the more critical attributes are built into the organization, the better will be the chances of success.

What is needed is for policymakers to decide on these questions in a step-wise fashion, taking three key questions in turn:

1. What influence should the President have on the activities of the MDO to ensure the public interest and future success in the siting of the facilities while allowing the MDO the flexibility to carry out its responsibilities?
2. How insulated from and independent of congressional oversight should the MDO be while ensuring public accountability?
3. How should the MDO be structured (through board membership, advisory committees, or other mechanisms to involve stakeholders and the public) to increase the likelihood of instilling public trust and attracting interest, engagement, and commitment of states, communities, and tribes in the siting of the facilities?

In answering these questions, policymakers will be striking a balance between the competing values of accountability and flexibility called for in the design of the new MDO.

---

[5]   Lee, 2003.

Comparison of the Tennessee Valley Authority and the Bonneville Power Administration

In this appendix, we describe two real-world examples of organizations that blend the features of private corporations and government agencies: TVA, a GOVCORP, and BPA, a government agency reporting to the Secretary of Energy.[1] The BRC referred to these organizations as possible models for an MDO. See Table A.1 for a comparison of the characteristics of these two organizations.

The Tennessee Valley Authority

TVA goes back to 1933, as part of President Franklin Delano Roosevelt's New Deal package of legislative reforms for responding to the Great Depression. TVA is probably best known for generating and selling electrical power and for building and operating large-scale engineering projects, including dams and nuclear power plants. It was also originally formed with the intent of using technology to help bring economic development to the Tennessee Valley, then a rural and impoverished region of the United States. Significant responsibilities and functions of TVA during its history have included flood control, maintaining navigation, rural electrification, fertilizer manufacturing, agricultural consulting, reforestation, and malaria prevention, as well as economic development and "integrated resource management." According to data published in TVA's 2011 annual report, the corporation currently has about 13,000 employees, generates annual operating revenues of about $11.7 billion, and makes about $530 million in annual tax-equivalent payments to state and local governments in eight states. TVA currently operates three nuclear power plants and 29 hydroelectric dams, in addition to many other smaller facilities and projects.

---

[1] We appreciate the careful review of our analyses in this Appendix by TVA and BPA officials.

Table A.1
Comparison of the Tennessee Valley Authority and the Bonneville Power Administration

Characteristic	GOVCORP: TVA	Government Agency: BPA
Charter	Act of Congress	Act of Congress
Direct oversight	Nine-member board of directors	Secretary of Energy
Role of President and White House	President nominates board of directors "to reflect diversity and needs of TVA service area"; President appoints independent IG; OMB reviews strategic plan and annual management and financial reports Budget is included in U.S. government consolidated budget and financial statements	Secretary of Energy appoints BPA Administrator; OMB exercises general oversight but has no legal authority to direct the funds of the Administrator BPA budget is included in U.S. government consolidated budget (as a subchapter in the DOE chapter) and financial statements
Role of Congress	Senate confirms board of directors Oversight: House Committee on Transportation and Infrastructure, Senate Committee on Environment and Public Works; reviews strategic plan, annual management and financial reports, and IG reports GAO conducts audits	Oversight: House Committee on Natural Resources, Senate Committee on Energy and Natural Resources; generally one annual hearing before House committee GAO conducts audits Pacific northwest congressional delegation often serves as an ad hoc advisory group on BPA issues
Funding	Self-financed; funds expenses from revenue from its customers; does not receive annual appropriations	Self-financed; funds expenses from revenue from utilities; "self-sustaining" under the Budget Enforcement Act[a]; does not receive annual appropriations
Financial management	Independent auditor Independent IG Audit committee of the board of directors Files 10-Ks, 10-Qs, and 8-Ks with the SEC	Independent auditor DOE IG
Borrowing authority	Sells bonds to public and can draw on a $150 million credit arrangement with Treasury	Sells bonds to Treasury
Ownership of entity	U.S. government instrumentality, wholly owned by the U.S. government; debt is not backed by the full faith and credit of the U.S. government	U.S. government; debt is not backed by the full faith and credit of the U.S. government
Regulatory obligations	Subject to federal laws and regulations	Subject to federal laws and regulations
Legal liabilities	Subject to private civil court claims; not protected by sovereign immunity; can sue and be sued in its own name	Does not have sue-and-be-sued authority; FTCA and sovereign immunity apply
Personnel management, procurement, contracting	Exempted from federal laws relating to hiring of federal employees, procurement of supplies and services, and acquisition of land; can exercise power of eminent domain	Subject to federal civil service requirements; exempted from federal procurement laws and the FAR—has its own procurement authorities; can exercise power of eminent domain
Setting of utility rates	TVA Act gives board of directors authority to set electricity rates; some FERC oversight applies	Administrator sets rates; FERC approves rates; can be reviewed by U.S. Court of Appeals for the Ninth Circuit

Table A.1—Continued

Characteristic	GOVCORP: TVA	Government Agency: BPA
Role of stakeholders	Seven members of the nine-member board of directors must be legal residents of the TVA service area; all must possess expertise in management and be selected to represent the diversity of the TVA service area TVA Regional Resources Stewardship Council is a 20-member advisory board to TVA, selected to represent diverse stakeholders (e.g., recreational, environmental, business) with regard to the management of natural resources in the Tennessee Valley	Daily interactions with utilities, tribes, environmental groups, states, local governments, federal agencies, the province of British Columbia and its crown corporation utilities, on all business matters; receives advice every five years from an interstate compact, the Northwest Power and Conservation Council, on a fish and wildlife plan and a power plan

[a] Pub. L. 101-508, 1990.

Congressional Charter

TVA was established in 1933 pursuant to the Tennessee Valley Authority Act.[2] The act is more than 30 pages long and lays out in considerable detail the structure of TVA and its operating characteristics. The formal terms of TVA's charter and the basic structure and function of TVA can be amended only by Congress through legislative action. There is nevertheless considerable flexibility for TVA to operate within the scope of its charter.

Direct Oversight and Roles of the President and Congress

The President appoints the nine-member board of directors upon the advice and consent of the U.S. Senate. The TVA charter establishes several requirements for members of the board, including that they have relevant executive management experience and that "at least 7 [members] shall be legal residents of the service area of the Corporation." Although the TVA charter does not require formal board representation for any specified stakeholder groups, it does call for the President to consider the recommendations of various stakeholder groups when making board appointments and to select board members who "reflect the diversity . . . and needs of the service area of the Corporation."

The TVA charter defines the powers, responsibilities, and structure of the board of directors. Most notably, the TVA board is responsible for developing broad goals and policies for the corporation; for establishing long-range plans to achieve those goals; for ensuring that the goals are, in fact, achieved; for approving an annual budget; and for hiring (and firing) a CEO. The board also has the ultimate responsibility for setting electricity rates. Beyond establishing the structure of the board, the TVA charter also

---

[2]   The TVA charter is codified in the Tennessee Valley Authority Act of 1933, at 16 U.S.C. §§ 831 et seq.

includes lengthy provisions that define many of the powers and authorized functions of the corporation itself. These include specific provisions for building and operating dams, power plants, and other major facilities; for issuing bonds and for repaying debts; for distributing 5 percent of the gross proceeds from the sale of electricity to state and local governments in lieu of taxes; and for pursuing various other development and policy goals through its operations, including flood control, soil erosion control, and the promotion of scientific agriculture.

TVA's expenditures are generally covered by its own operating revenue, so TVA is therefore not subject to the ordinary congressional appropriations process. TVA is also not supervised by any executive branch officials, e.g., OMB or a department secretary.

TVA is subject to various financial and operational reporting requirements both to Congress and to the executive branch, based on the terms of the TVA charter and relevant provisions of the GCCA. OMB and Congress review TVA's strategic plans, as well as annual management and financial reports. Oversight is through the House Committee on Transportation and Infrastructure and the Senate Committee on Environment and Public Works.

Funding and Borrowing Authority

Although TVA has received congressional appropriations in the past, it is currently entirely funded from operating revenues through sales of electricity, through the sale of bonds in the financial markets, and through other power system financings. TVA can also draw on a $150 million credit agreement with the Treasury.

Ownership of Entity

TVA is a wholly owned U.S. government instrumentality. It does not issue equity securities or have any other (nongovernment) ownership or shareholders. According to the TVA Act, although TVA securities are "not backed by the full faith and credit of the United States," TVA is nevertheless a "corporate agency and instrumentality of the U.S. government."[3]

Regulatory Obligations

TVA's most recent annual 10-K report to the SEC offers a brief description of the regulatory oversight that currently applies to the corporation. Per the 10-K, TVA was explicitly exempted by Congress from "some general federal laws that apply to other agencies, such as . . . laws relating to the hiring of federal employees, the procurement of supplies and services, and the acquisition of land."[4]

---

[3]   See Pub L. 73-17 (1993); see also TVA, 2011b.

[4]   TVA, 2011b.

Notwithstanding, TVA does remain subject to various other areas of federal law and regulation, including environmental protection, civil rights, and conservation of cultural resources.

Again according to TVA's form 10-K, the corporation is required to file periodic reports with the SEC under section 37 of the Securities Exchange Act of 1934, even though TVA is exempt from many other requirements of the federal securities laws because of its status as an agency and instrumentality of the U.S. government.[5] TVA notably also meets the statutory definition of an "electric utility" and "transmitting utility" under the Federal Power Act of 1935, and therefore is subject to some aspects of the regulatory jurisdiction exercised by FERC.[6]

Legal Liabilities

GOVCORPs generally are subject to, and may initiate, their own civil claims. By implication, most GOVCORPs are not protected from suit by sovereign immunity, despite the fact that they are nevertheless considered agencies and instrumentalities of the U.S. government. TVA clearly follows the general pattern in this regard. According to TVA's most recent annual financial statements, in the preceding year the corporation had "accrued approximately $391 million of potential losses with respect to legal proceedings through September 30, 2011." The financial statements go on to enumerate a lengthy set of pending civil claims and matters involving TVA, including litigation related to Hurricane Katrina; to multiple pollution-related disputes with EPA and conservation groups; to NRC regulatory oversight and licensing activities for current and proposed TVA facilities; to disparate public nuisance and other tort claims involving air pollution and greenhouse-gas emissions from TVA power plants; and to a dispute concerning fiduciary oversight for the TVA retirement system.

Personnel Management, Procurement, and Contracting

TVA is exempted from federal laws relating to the hiring of federal employees, procurement of supplies and services, and acquisition of land.

TVA specifies that, in compensating its staff, it needs to take into account compensation for similar positions in private industry, public utilities, and state and federal governments. In its 2012 report to Congress, TVA stated that, although it no longer receives federal payments, it nevertheless "viewed the language and intent of the legislative freeze on federal employees" proposed by the administration and approved by Congress, and "applied the [same] principles to its executives and managers."[7] In its financial management, TVA has both an independent auditor and independent IG.

---

[5]   Pub. L. 73-291, Securities Exchange Act, 1934.

[6]   49 Stat. 863, Federal Power Act, 1935.

[7]   TVA, 2011a, p. 6.

Role of Stakeholders

As described earlier, the TVA charter specifically directs the President to select the members of the TVA board with an eye toward representing the diversity and needs of the service area of the corporation (i.e., the Tennessee Valley region). To some degree, then, the TVA board itself provides an element of stakeholder engagement, although less so than in an organization in which different stakeholder groups have the immediate opportunity to appoint their own representatives to the governing board.

According to various historical summaries describing TVA, the corporation encountered significant skepticism and controversy in its early years of operation, in part because its mission involved going into a very underdeveloped region of the United States, and convincing large numbers of people to modify their farming practices and to participate in rural electrification and environmental conservation projects. Moreover, some of TVA's flood-control and dam-building activities may have involved the necessity of relocating homeowners, at least occasionally without their consent.

TVA today describes itself as continuously seeking opportunities for stakeholder engagement, both formal and informal. One recent example of this reportedly involved TVA's creation of a created a Stakeholder Review Group as part of its 2011 Integrated Resource Plan process, which also included opportunities for public input. In addition, TVA has continued to seek public input through its Regional Resource Stewardship Council, a TVA advisory group that serves to "provide recommendations and advice to TVA on the agency's stewardship activities [and] on TVA's public participation efforts." The council includes up to 20 members, with seven seats directly appointed by the governors of Alabama, Georgia, Kentucky, Mississippi, North Carolina, Tennessee, and Virginia. The remaining 13 seats on the council can be filled at the discretion of the TVA governing board, with the aim of ensuring that "membership is balanced, and that it represents and includes a broad range of diverse views and interests, including recreational, environmental, industrial, business, consumer, educational, and community leadership interests."[8]

The Bonneville Power Administration

BPA is a U.S. federal nonprofit agency that aims to (1) provide "adequate, efficient, economical and reliable power supply" to the Pacific Northwest region; (2) ensure a reliable and stable transmission system; and (3) "mitigate the Federal Columbia River Power system's impact on fish and wildlife."[9] BPA was established in 1937 by the Bonneville Project Act to market the power generated from Bonneville Dam.[10] According to

---

[8]   TVA, 2009.

[9]   See BPA, 2011a.

[10]   50 Stat. 731, Bonneville Project Act, 1937.

President Franklin Roosevelt, the construction of the Bonneville Dam was to ensure that "the next great federal hydroelectric project would be built on the Columbia River to prevent extortion against the public by the giant electric utility holding companies then dominant in the region."[11] Thirty-one federal dams now make up the federal hydroelectric system. BPA owns and operates one of the nation's largest high-voltage transmission systems, and uses it to deliver electrical power from federal and nonfederal power generation units. As a self-financed, separate and distinct entity within DOE, BPA supplies 40 percent of the electric power used in the Pacific Northwest region through wholesaling of electrical power generated from federal hydroelectric projects along the Columbia River Basin, one nonfederal nuclear power plant, and several other small nonfederal power plants.[12] BPA carries the legal obligation to sell electrical power produced by the Federal Columbia River Power Systems (FCRPS) at cost to any utility in the region with preference to public power. BPA currently has approximately 3,100 employees, owns and operates 15,215 circuit-miles of transmission line, and generates annual operating revenues of $3.3 billion (combined accounts under the FCRPS).[13]

Congressional Charter

BPA was established in 1937 by the Bonneville Project Act, which provided the statutory foundation of BPA's obligations and authorities. The 1974 Federal Columbia River Transmission System Act placed BPA under the provisions of the GCCA that authorized BPA to self-finance and allow it to (1) use revenues generated from the selling of electric power and transmission ratepayers to direct fund all programs and (2) to "sell bonds to the Treasury to finance the region's high voltage electric transmission system requirements."[14] The enactment of the 1980 Northwest Power Act added three extra obligations to BPA: "encourage electric energy conservation; when resource acquisition is necessary, give priority to resources which are cost-effective and then in the following order: conservation, renewable, waste heat or high fuel conversion efficiency, and all others; and protect, mitigate and enhance the fish and wildlife of the Columbia River and its tributaries."[15] BPA was then allowed to sell bonds to finance "conservation and other resources and to carry out fish and wildlife capital improvements."[16]

---

[11] See BPA, undated.

[12] See BPA, 2011a.

[13] BPA, 2011d, "Management's Discussion and Analysis," p. 4.

[14] DOE, 2010b, p. 145; Pub. L. 93-454, Federal Columbia River Transmission System Act, 1974; 31 U.S.C. §§ 9101–9110.

[15] Pub. L. 96-501, 1980; see also 16 U.S.C. 839b.

[16] DOE, 2010b, p. 145.

Direct Oversight and Roles of the President and Congress

As a government agency, BPA has neither shareholders nor a board of directors. The Bonneville Project Act established a position of administrator, which is appointed by and reports to the Secretary of Energy. The administrator is in charge of "the overall planning, development, and administration of policies that govern the operation of a large public utility."[17] The administrator can "make arrangements for the sale and disposition of electric energy"; decide on the installation and maintenance of machinery, equipment, and facilities; and ensure the implementation of environment-, health-, and safety-related responsibilities. Under established BPA policies and applicable regulations, the administrator and deputy administrator do not engage in direct, day-to-day supervision of "merchant power function activities" but instead delegate those activities to their subordinates within BPA.[18] Although BPA has no formal board of directors, the Pacific Northwest congressional delegation typically acts an informal, ad hoc oversight and advisory board.

The BPA budget is part of the administration's financial statement to Congress. Under the relevant provisions of the GCCA, BPA prepares and submits a business-type budget to the President each year.[19] The Congress reviews and approves BPA's annual budget. Programmatic activities are also subject to congressional review and oversights, e.g., through GAO and the Comptroller General. Accounts and financial performances of BPA are reviewed by OMB and an independent third-party auditor. The IG of DOE also reviews BPA's activities. The U.S. House of Representatives Committee on Natural Resources Subcommittee on Water and Power has jurisdiction over BPA.[20] The administrator testifies on the budget in front of the committee every year. BPA is also under the jurisdiction of U.S. Senate Committee of Energy and Natural Resources Subcommittee on Water and Power.[21]

Funding, Financial Management, and Borrowing Authority

BPA is a self-funded agency and does not receive an annual congressional appropriation. Under the Transmission System Act, BPA funds its expenses with revenues from electric power and transmission rates. All cash flows go into one account (the BPA Fund) at the Treasury.[22] BPA sells power generated from the federal power system

---

[17] BPA, 2007.

[18] Per BPA, 2011c, the BPA administrator and deputy administrator are classified as shared senior officers under FERC standards of conduct. And, per BPA, 2010c, the FERC rules stipulate that "Shared Senior Officers [will] not engage in day-to-day actions . . . that direct, organize, or execute transmission or merchant power function activities, except in emergency circumstances affecting transmission system reliability."

[19] BPA, 2010b, p. 147.

[20] Wright, 2012.

[21] U.S. Senate Committee on Energy and Natural Resources, undated.

[22] Moody's Investor Services, 2011, p. 4.

primarily through long-term contracts to its customers, which are mainly consumer-owned utilities in Idaho, western Montana, Oregon, and Washington. If the federal power system generates power beyond BPA's commitment, BPA can sell these surpluses or secondary power to other customers in the Pacific Northwest or western states. BPA typically sells this secondary power at market price. BPA must submit its power and transmission rates to FERC for final approval.

As a self-financed government agency, BPA does not issue stock to finance its capital investments. BPA generally finances its capital investments through federal financed Treasury debt. BPA can have, at most, $7.7 billion of debt with the U.S. Treasury at any time.

As a federal agency, BPA cannot borrow directly from nonfederal sources. However, it may and has secured third-party financing from time to time.

Ownership of Entity

BPA is a wholly owned U.S. government agency. It does not issue equity securities or have any other (nongovernment) ownership or shareholders.

Regulatory Obligations

The compliance and governance activities unit within BPA ensures BPA's compliance with numerous areas of governmental regulation, including those promulgated by DOE, OMB, and FERC.[23] Although BPA's transmission system is reportedly outside of FERC's jurisdiction, BPA nevertheless voluntarily complies with certain FERC orders pertaining to transmission systems.[24]

Several major federal statutes contain regulatory provisions specifically applying to BPA. These include the Bonneville Project Act, Federal Columbia River Transmission System Act, Pacific Northwest Electric Power Planning and Conservation Act, and the National Environmental Policy Act.[25] However, BPA is notably exempted from the Gramm-Rudman-Hollings Balanced Budget and Emergency Deficit Control Act of 1985.[26] The submission of BPA's annual report fulfills the reporting requirements of the Third Powerplant at Grand Coulee Dam Act.[27] BPA is also subject to the

---

[23] BPA's financial systems and processes must meet the requirement of OMB, 1999, 2003, and of OMB, Treasury, and GAO Core Financial System Requirements, per BPA, 2010d. BPA is also subject to the FERC standards of conduct, codified at 18 C.F.R. §§ 358.5(a)(1)–(2) (2006), which require that "transmission services/function must function independently from power services to prevent transmission providers from providing information to power marketing employees that may hurt other transmission customers." See BPA, 2010a.

[24] GAO, 2004, pp. 8–9.

[25] 42 U.S.C. § 4321.

[26] BPA, 2005.

[27] BPA, 2011d, "Management's Discussion and Analysis"; Pub. L. 89-448, Third Powerplant at Grand Coulee Dam Act, 1966.

electric reliability standards promulgated by the North American Electric Reliability Corporation.

In addition, because BPA is obligated to "protect, mitigate, and enhance fish and wildlife in the Columbia River Basin," these actions are guided by a list of federal laws and regulations, such as the Endangered Species Act, treaties with tribal governments, and various relevant President's executive orders.[28]

Legal Liabilities

Because BPA guaranteed the bonds issued by Energy Northwest, it is now responsible for the nonfederal debt associated with two non-operating nuclear plants and one operating nuclear plant, the Columbia Generating Station. BPA is required by statute to defer its annual U.S. Treasury repayment if it needs to meet nonfederal debt service commitments (such as Energy Northwest bonds) under the net billing agreements.[29]

In general, BPA faces civil liability risk in a manner similar to other independent government agencies and PMAs. As noted in Table A.1 above, BPA does not have its own sue-and-be-sued authority, and the provisions of the FTCA and sovereign immunity doctrine do apply to the agency. The U.S. Department of Justice is responsible for management and oversight of BPA litigation.

The Northwest Power Act requires BPA to provide a subsidy for the residential and small-farm customers of investor-owned utilities, to provide equity between their rates and the rates of consumer-owned utilities. Disputes and civil litigation related to this program eventually led to a major settlement agreement, under which BPA agreed to pay more than $3B in long-term liabilities.[30]

Role of Stakeholders

Given its span of responsibilities and associated assets, BPA must engage a wide variety of stakeholders on a sustained basis. It must report to DOE leadership and to a variety of BPA customers (including consumer-owned utilities, investor-owned utilities, direct service industries, and customers outside the northwest consisting of consumer-owned and investor-owned utilities in the southwest and California). It must also engage tribes. In addition to supplying tribal utilities, it has treaty and non-treaty tribal policies that must be followed in cases in which BPA actions may affect tribal resources:

> BPA, the Corps and Reclamation signed historic 10-year agreements, known as the Columbia Basin Fish Accords, with five Columbia Basin Indian tribes and two states in 2008. In 2009, Agreements were signed with another tribe, state, and federal agencies. These agreements provide specific hydro, habitat, hatchery and

---

[28] BPA, 2009.

[29] Moody's Investor Services, 2011, p. 4.

[30] BPA, 2011d, "Audited Financial Statements," pp. 20–22.

other measures that will address recovery needs and provide measurable biological benefits for fish.[31]

Its importance to the Pacific Northwest region also brought BPA strong political constituencies on key U.S. House and Senate committees. Several U.S. senators from the region are on the Senate Energy and Natural Resources Committee, which deals with legislation related to BPA.[32]

Long-term power planning for the Pacific Northwest is the responsibility of the Northwest Power and Conservation Council. The Northwest Power and Conservation Council was authorized in the Northwest Power Act of 1980 and approved by a vote of the legislatures of all four states: Idaho, Montana, Oregon, and Washington. The governor of each state appoints two members to serve on the council.[33] The adopted power plan must be submitted to Congress and reviewed by the council at least every five years. BPA acquisition of power generating resources must align with the power plan developed by the Northwest Power and Conservation Council. Thus, this regional council provides stakeholder advice in BPA's service area.

---

[31] DOE, 2010b, pp. 151–152.

[32] Moody's Investor Services, 2011, p. 6.

[33] Northwest Power and Conservation Council, undated.

Summary of Organizational Characteristics of Canadian and Swedish MDOs

Canada and Sweden are examples of nations that have chosen to form MDOs based on private, nongovernment forms of organization. Canada's Nuclear Waste Management Organization (NWMO) is a nonprofit private organization established by statute. The Swedish Nuclear Fuel and Waste Management Company (SKB) is a for-profit organization. Both are nongovernmental organizations formed by nuclear utilities, funded by fees drawn from those utilities, and subject to extensive government mandates and regulatory oversight. Both NWMO and SKB have been the focus of multiple previous case studies complied by IAEA, NWTRB, DOE, and others.[1] Our own review and tabular presentation of some of the basic features of these organizations is largely based on these earlier case studies and reviews.

The NWMO is different from the PRIVCORP model discussed in Chapter Three to the extent that it has a nonprofit orientation; indeed, as a nonprofit, its legislative charter looks more like the GOVCORP model.[2] Both NWMO and SKB are not entirely private, however. As noted by NWTRB, "[s]ome of the Canadian and Swedish utilities that own the implementing organizations are partly government-owned."[3] Each organization has adapted a variation of a phased adaptive management approach to siting. Finally, it is worth noting that the design of each organization is a product of previously failed national approaches to achieve consent on siting.

---

[1] Swedish Nuclear Fuel and Waste Management Company, undated, 2012; IAEA, 2007; Nuclear Waste Management Organization, undated, 2012; Canada, Nuclear Fuel Waste Act of 2002, Bill C-27; NWTRB, 2009, 2011; Organisation for Economic Co-operation and Development, 2011; World Nuclear Association, undated; International Association for Environmentally Safe Disposal of Radioactive Materials, 2005.

[2] Canada, Nuclear Fuel Waste Act of 2002.

[3] NWTRB, 2011, p. 18.

Table B.1
Major Characteristics of Canadian and Swedish MDOs

Characteristic	Canada (NWMO)	Sweden (SKB)
Type of organization	Private, nonprofit corporation	Private, for-profit corporation
Implementing organization	Nuclear Waste Management Organization	Swedish Nuclear Fuel and Waste Management Company
Creation	NWMO mandated by legislation (Nuclear Fuel Waste Act of 2002), established by nuclear energy utilities	Responsibility to manage nuclear waste mandated by legislation, organization formed by licensees holding nuclear waste
Direct oversight	Board of Directors appointed by nuclear energy utilities	Board of Directors appointed by nuclear waste licensees
Role of government	Regular review and approval of assessments and major decisions	Regular review and approval of assessments and major decisions, including siting
Funding	All costs covered by a trust fund with fees paid by nuclear energy utilities through a government-approved formula; only NWMO has authority to withdraw from the account	Nuclear Waste Fund, funded by fees paid by nuclear waste licensees; fund is managed by a government board
Financial management	Auditing by private, third-party (Deloitte)	Government auditing
Borrowing authority	Funding available; no borrowing required	Funding available; no borrowing required
Owners/founders of entity	Jointly founded by nuclear energy utilities, pursuant to legislative mandate	Jointly owned by nuclear utility licensees
Regulatory authority	Canadian Nuclear Safety Commission	Swedish Radiation Safety Authority (SSM), Swedish National Council for Nuclear Waste (formerly known as KASAM)
Legal liabilities	NWMO has full liability	SKB has full liability
Personnel management, procurement contracting	No special requirements	No special requirements
Site selection	Voluntary process; environmental assessment must be approved by the Federal Minister of the Environment	Voluntary process; applications must be approved by the Swedish Radiation Safety Authority (SSM) and the Environmental Court
Licensing	Canadian Nuclear Safety Commission has full authority, no further government action required	Government grants permission, and a nonbinding vote of Parliament may occur

List of Mixed-Ownership Government Corporations and Wholly Owned Government Corporations

In 31 U.S.C. § 9101, the GCCA provides lists of mixed-ownership government corporations and wholly owned government corporations.

Mixed-Ownership Government Corporations

The mixed-ownership government corporations are as follows:

- Central Bank for Cooperatives
- Federal Deposit Insurance Corporation
- Federal Home Loan Banks
- Federal Intermediate Credit Bank
- Federal Land Bank
- National Credit Union Administration Central Liquidity Facility
- Regional Banks for Cooperatives
- Rural Telephone Bank when the ownership, control, and operation of the bank are converted
- Financing Corporation
- Resolution Trust Corporation
- Resolution Funding Corporation.

Wholly Owned Government Corporations

The wholly owned government corporations are as follows:

- Commodity Credit Corporation
- Community Development Financial Institutions Fund
- Export-Import Bank of the United States
- Federal Crop Insurance Corporation

- Federal Prison Industries, Inc.
- Corporation for National and Community Service
- Government National Mortgage Association
- Overseas Private Investment Corporation
- Pennsylvania Avenue Development Corporation
- Pension Benefit Guaranty Corporation
- Rural Telephone Bank [until the ownership, control, and operation of the bank are converted]
- Saint Lawrence Seaway Development Corporation
- Secretary of Housing and Urban Development (when carrying out duties and powers related to the Federal Housing Administration Fund)
- Tennessee Valley Authority
- Panama Canal Commission
- Millennium Challenge Corporation
- International Clean Energy Foundation.

References

Advisory Panel on Alternative Means of Financing and Managing Radioactive Waste Facilities, *Managing Nuclear Waste: A Better Idea—A Report to the U.S. Secretary of Energy*, Washington, D.C., December 1984. As of April 23, 2012:
http://brc.gov/sites/default/files/documents/amfm_1984_s.pdf

Aluminum Co. of America v Central Lincoln Peoples' Utility Dist., 467 U.S. 380, 104 S. Ct. 2472, June 5, 1984.

AMFM—*See* Advisory Panel on Alternative Means of Financing and Managing Radioactive Waste Facilities.

Arnold Tours, Inc. v Camp, 472 F. 2d 427, 1st Cir., December 13, 1972.

Association of Data Processing Service Organization, Inc. v Federal Home Loan Bank Board, 568 F. 2d 478, 6th Cir., December 5, 1977.

Blue Ribbon Commission on America's Nuclear Future, *Report to the Secretary of Energy*, Washington, D.C., January 2012. As of April 23, 2012:
http://purl.fdlp.gov/GPO/gpo20637

Board of Governors of the Federal Reserve System, *The Federal Reserve System: Purposes and Functions*, Washington, D.C.: Federal Reserve Board, 2005. As of April 26, 2012:
http://www.federalreserve.gov/pf/pf.htm

Boin, Arjen, Sanneke Kuipers, and Marco Steenbergen, "The Life and Death of Public Organizations: A Question of Institutional Design?" *Governance*, Vol. 23, No. 3, July 2010, pp. 385–410.

Bonneville Power Administration, "About BPA: A History of Service," undated. As of April 19, 2012:
http://www.bpa.gov/power/pl/columbia/1-hist.htm

———, *BPA Manual*, sections dated August 2004–September 2011. As of April 23, 2012:
http://www.bpa.gov/EBR/BPAManual/bpam.htm

———, "BPA Statutes," updated July 29, 2005. As of April 19, 2012:
http://www.bpa.gov/Corporate/KC/statutes/statutes.shtml

———, "Functional Statement for Office of the Administrator and Chief Executive Officer," *BPA Manual*, August 14, 2007. As of April 24, 2012:
http://www.bpa.gov/EBR/BPAManual/toc.htm

———, Environment, Fish and Wildlife, "Legal Framework: Laws, Treaties, and Executive Orders," last reviewed November 4, 2009. As of April 19, 2012:
http://efw.bpa.gov/IntegratedFWP/legalframework.aspx

———, Transmission, "FERC Standards of Conduct," last modified May 4, 2010a. As of April 19, 2012:
http://transmission.bpa.gov/soc/

———, *BPA Statutes*, June 2010b. As of April 19, 2012:
http://www.bpa.gov/corporate/docs/BPA-Statutes.pdf

———, "Delegations of Authority to Bind the Agency," *BPA Manual*, August 20, 2010c. As of April 24, 2012:
http://www.bpa.gov/EBR/BPAManual/toc.htm

———, "Internal Controls Protocols and Actions," *BPA Manual*, August 20, 2010d. As of April 24, 2012:
http://www.bpa.gov/EBR/BPAManual/toc.htm

———, "2010 BPA Facts," April 2011. As of April 19, 2012:
http://www.bpa.gov/corporate/about_BPA/Facts/FactDocs/BPA_Facts_2010.pdf

———, "Functional Statement for Office of the Deputy Administrator," *BPA Manual*, September 9, 2011c. As of April 24, 2012:
http://www.bpa.gov/EBR/BPAManual/toc.htm

———, *2011 Annual Report*, November 2011d. As of April 19, 2012:
http://www.bpa.gov/corporate/Finance/A_Report/

Bowsher v Synar, 478 U.S. 714, 106 S. Ct. 3181, July 7, 1986.

BPA—*See* Bonneville Power Administration.

BRC—*See* Blue Ribbon Commission on America's Nuclear Future.

Breger, Marshall J., and Gary J. Edles, "Established by Practice: The Theory and Operation of Independent Federal Agencies," *Administrative Law Review*, Vol. 52, No. 4, Fall 2000, pp. 1111–1294.

Canada, Nuclear Fuel Waste Act of 2002, Bill C-27. As of May 3, 2012:
http://www.parl.gc.ca/HousePublications/Publication.aspx?Pub=Bill&Doc=C-27&Language=E&Mode=1&Parl=37&Ses=1&File=6

Cavinato, Joseph L., and Ralph G. Kauffman, *The Purchasing Handbook: A Guide for the Purchasing and Supply Professional*, Sixth Edition, Tempe, Ariz.: National Association of Purchasing Management, 2000.

C.F.R—*See* Code of Federal Regulations.

Code of Federal Regulations, Title 18, Conservation of power and water resources, Chapter I, Federal Energy Regulatory Commission, Department of Energy, Subchapter S, Standards of conduct for transmission providers, Part 358, Standards of conduct, Section 358.5, Independent functioning rule.

———, Title 48, Federal Acquisition Regulations System, Chapter 1, Federal Acquisition Regulation, Subchapter A, General, Part 2, Definitions of words and terms, Subpart 2.1, Definitions.

Devia v NRC, 492 F. 3d 421, 377 U.S. App. D.C. 122 (D.C. Cir., June 26, 2007).

Devins, Neal, and David E. Lewis, "Not-So Independent Agencies: Party Polarization and the Limits of Institutional Design," *Boston University Law Review*, Vol. 88, 2008, pp. 459–498.

Dockery v Federal Deposit Insurance Corp., 64 M.S.P.R. 458, 460–462, 1994.

DOE—*See* U.S. Department of Energy.

Easterling, Douglas, and Howard Kunreuther, *The Dilemma of Siting a High-Level Nuclear Waste Depository*, Boston, Mass.: Kluwer Academic Publishers, 1995.

Elson, Charles M., "Director Compensation and the Management-Captured Board: The History of a Symptom and a Cure," *Southern Methodist University Law Review*, Vol. 50, No. 1, September–October 1996, p. 127–174.

EPA—*See* U.S. Environmental Protection Agency.

Federal Land Bank v Bismarck Lumber Co., 314 U.S. 95, 62 S. Ct. 1, November 10, 1941.

Fertel, Marvin S., Testimony before the U.S. House of Representatives Appropriations Subcommittee on Energy and Water Development, Washington, D.C., March 19, 2010.

Fischhoff, Baruch, "'Acceptable Risk': The Case of Nuclear Power," *Journal of Policy Analysis and Management*, Vol. 2, No. 4, 1983, pp. 559–575.

Fischhoff, Baruch, Paul Slovic, Sarah Lichtenstein, Stephen Read, and Barbara Combs, "How Safe Is Safe Enough? A Psychometric Study of Attitudes Towards Technological Risks and Benefits," *Policy Sciences*, Vol. 9, 1978, pp. 127–152.

Forsberg, Charles, "Integrating Repositories with Fuel Cycles: The Airport Authority Model," *Proceedings of ICAPP '12*, Chicago, Ill.: American Nuclear Society, paper 12007, June 2012.

Froomkin, A. Michael, "Reinventing the Government Corporation," *University of Illinois Law Review*, Vol. 543, No. 3, 1995, pp. 543–634.

Fund for Animals v Babbitt, 903 F. Supp. 96, D.D.C., September 29, 1995, amended, 967 F. Supp. 6, D.D.C., 1997.

GAO—*See* U.S. General Accounting Office (until 2004) or U.S. Government Accountability Office (after 2004).

IAEA—*See* International Atomic Energy Agency.

International Association for Environmentally Safe Disposal of Radioactive Materials, *Report on Radioactive Waste Ownership and Management of Long-Term Liabilities in EDRAM Member Countries*, June 2005. As of May 3, 2012:
http://www.edram.info/fileadmin/edram/pdf/EDRAMWGonWOwnershipFinal_271005.pdf

International Atomic Energy Agency, *Factors Affecting Public and Political Acceptance for the Implementation of Geological Disposal*, Vienna, IAEA-TECDOC-1566, October 2007.

Kosar, Kevin R., *Government-Sponsored Enterprises (GSEs): An Institutional Overview*, Washington, D.C.: Congressional Research Service, RS21663, April 23, 2007.

———, *Federal Government Corporations: An Overview*, Washington, D.C.: Congressional Research Service, RL30365, June 8, 2011.

La Porte, Todd R., and Ann Keller, "Assuring Institutional Constancy: Requisite for Managing Long-Lived Hazards," *Public Administration Review*, Vol. 56, No. 6, November–December 1996, pp. 535–544.

La Porte, Todd R., and Daniel S. Metlay, "Hazards and Institutional Trustworthiness: Facing a Deficit of Trust," *Public Administration Review*, Vol. 56, No. 4, July–August 1996, pp. 341–347.

Lebron v Nat'l R.R. Passenger Corp., 513 U.S. 374, 115 S. Ct. 961, February 21, 1995.

Lee, Kai N., *Adaptive Management in the Canadian Nuclear Waste Program*, Nuclear Waste Management Organization Background Paper, 2003.

Lewis, David E., *Presidents and the Politics of Agency Design: Political Insulation in the United States Government Bureaucracy, 1946–1997*, Stanford, Calif.: Stanford University Press, 2003.

Macfarlane, Allison, and Rodney C. Ewing, eds., *Uncertainty Underground: Yucca Mountain and the Nation's High-Level Nuclear Waste*, Cambridge, Mass.: MIT Press, 2006.

McCubbins, Matthew D., Roger D. Noll, and Barry R. Weingast, "Structure and Process, Politics and Policy: Administrative Arrangements and the Political Control of Agencies," *Virginia Law Review*, Vol. 75, No. 2, March 1989, pp. 431–482.

McCulloch v Md., 17 U.S. 316, March 6, 1819.

Merrow, Edward W., *Industrial Megaprojects: Concepts, Strategies, and Practices for Success*, Hoboken, N.J.: Wiley, 2011.

Moody's Investor Services, "Energy Northwest: Bonneville Power Administration," June 3, 2011. As of April 19, 2012:
http://www.bpa.gov/corporate/Finance/Debt_Management/reports_articles/docs/2011/Moody_sMay.pdf

National Academy of Public Administration, *Deciding for the Future: Balancing Risks, Costs, and Benefits Fairly Across Generations—A Report*, Washington, D.C., June 1997.

National Commission on the BP Deepwater Horizon Oil Spill and Offshore Drilling, *Deep Water: The Gulf Oil Disaster and the Future of Offshore Drilling—Report to the President*, Washington, D.C., 2011. As of April 24, 2012:
http://purl.fdlp.gov/GPO/gpo2978

Northwest Power and Conservation Council, "Background," undated. As of April 19, 2012:
http://www.nwcouncil.org/about/background.htm

Nuclear Waste Management Organization (Canada), website, undated. As of May 2, 2012:
http://www.nwmo.ca/home?language=en_CA

———, *Learning More Together: Annual Report 2011*, 2012.

"Nuclear Waste Negotiator Office," *Federal Register*, undated. As of April 26, 2012:
https://www.federalregister.gov/agencies/nuclear-waste-negotiator-office

NWTRB—*See* U.S. Nuclear Waste Technical Review Board.

Office of Management and Budget, *Financial Management Systems*, Washington, D.C., Circular A-127, June 10, 1999. As of April 19, 2012:
http://purl.access.gpo.gov/GPO/LPS46092

———, *Performance of Commercial Activities*, Washington, D.C., Circular A-76, 2003. As of April 19, 2012:
http://purl.access.gpo.gov/GPO/LPS45892

Organisation for Economic Co-operation and Development, "Actual Implementation of a Spent Nuclear Fuel Repository in Sweden: Seizing Opportunities," Radioactive Waste Management Committee, Synthesis of the FSC National Workshop and Community Visit, Osthammer, Sweden, May 4–6, 2011.

Osborn v President, Directors and Co. of Bank, 22 U.S. 738, March 19, 1824.

Pittman v Home Owners' Loan Corp., 308 U.S. 21, November 6, 1939.

Public Law 73-17, Tennessee Valley Authority Act of 1933, May 18, 1933.

Public Law 73-291, Securities Exchange Act of 1934, June 6, 1934.

Public Law 85-256, Price-Anderson Act, September 2, 1957.

Public Law 87-26, Communications Satellite Act of 1962, April 25, 1961.

Public Law 89-448, Third Powerplant at Grand Coulee Dam Act, June 14, 1966.

Public Law 91-518, Rail Passenger Service Act of 1970, October 30, 1970.

Public Law 93-205, Endangered Species Act of 1973, December 28, 1973.

Public Law 93-400, Office of Federal Procurement Policy Act, August 30, 1974.

Public Law 93-454, Federal Columbia River Transmission System Act of 1974, October 18, 1974.

Public Law 96-501, Pacific Northwest Electric Power Planning and Conservation Act, December 5, 1980.

Public Law 97-425, Nuclear Waste Policy Act of 1982, January 7, 1983.

Public Law 99-177, Gramm-Rudman-Hollings Balanced Budget and Emergency Deficit Control Act of 1985, December 12, 1985.

Public Law 100-202, Nuclear Waste Policy Act Amendment, December 22, 1987.

Public Law 100-203, Nuclear Waste Policy Act Amendment, December 22, 1987.

Public Law 101-508, Budget Enforcement Act of 1990, November 5, 1990.

Public Law 111-314, National Aeronautics and Space Act, December 18, 2010.

Reagan, Ronald, letter to Secretary of Energy John S. Herrington, "Disposal of Defense Waste in a Commercial Repository," Washington, D.C., April 30, 1985.

Review Group, *Report to the Secretary of Energy on the Conclusions and Recommendations of the Advisory Panel on Alternative Means of Financing and Managing (AMFM) Radioactive Waste Management Facilities*, Washington, D.C.: U.S. Department of Energy, April 18, 1985. As of April 23, 2012:
http://brc.gov/sites/default/files/documents/amfm_doe_response_s.pdf

SEAB—*See* Secretary of Energy Advisory Board.

Secretary of Energy Advisory Board, *Earning Public Trust and Confidence: Requisites for Managing Radioactive Wastes—Final Report*, Washington, D.C.: U.S. Department of Energy, 1993. As of April 26, 2012:
http://www.osti.gov/bridge/servlets/purl/10184724-j8WVKp/webviewable/10184724.pdf

Slovic, Paul, Baruch Fischhoff, and Sarah Lichtenstein, "Facts Versus Fears: Understanding Perceived Risk," in Daniel Kahneman, Paul Slovic, and Amos Tversky, eds., *Judgment Under Uncertainty: Heuristics and Biases*, Cambridge, UK: Cambridge University Press, 1982.

Stewart, Richard B., "U.S. Nuclear Waste Law and Policy: Fixing a Bankrupt System," *N.Y.U. Environmental Law Journal*, Vol. 17, 2008, pp. 783–825.

Swedish Nuclear Fuel and Waste Management Company, website, undated. As of May 2, 2012:
http://www.skb.se/default____24417.aspx

———, *Activities 2011*, 2012.

Tennessee Valley Authority, "Regional Council Charter," effective February 2, 2009. As of April 19, 2012:
http://www.tva.gov/rrsc/rrsc_charter.htm

————, *Budget Proposal and Management Agenda, for the Fiscal Year Ending September 30, 2012, Submitted to Congress February 2011*, Knoxville, Tenn., February 2011a. As of April 19, 2012:
http://www.tva.com/abouttva/pdf/budget_proposal_2012.pdf

————, form 10-K, November 17, 2011b.

Truman, Harry S., "Annual Budget Message to the Congress: Fiscal Year 1948," Washington, D.C., January 10, 1947. As of April 19, 2012:
http://www.trumanlibrary.org/publicpapers/index.php?pid=2046&st=&st1=

Tuler, Seth P., and Roger E. Kasperson, *Social Distrust: Implications and Recommendation for Spent Nuclear Fuel and High Level Radioactive Waste Management: A Technical Report Prepared for the Blue Ribbon Commission on America's Nuclear Future*, Washington, D.C.: Blue Ribbon Commission on America's Nuclear Future, 2010.

TVA—*See* Tennessee Valley Authority.

U.S. Code, Title 5, Government organization and employees, Part I, The agencies generally, Chapter 1, Organization, Section 103, Government corporation.

————, Title 5, Government organization and employees, Part III, Employees, Subpart B, Employment and retention, Chapter 31, Authority for employment, Subchapter II, The senior executive service, Section 3132, Definitions and exclusions.

————, Title 5, Government organization and employees, Part III, Employees, Subpart C, Employee performance, Chapter 43, Performance appraisal, Subchapter I, General provisions, Section 4301, Definitions.

————, Title 5, Government organization and employees, Part III, Employees, Subpart D, Pay and allowances, Chapter 51, Classification, Section 5102, Definitions; application.

————, Title 5, Government organization and employees, Part III, Employees, Subpart D, Pay and allowances, Chapter 53, Pay rates and systems, Subchapter III, General schedule pay rates, Section 5331, Definitions; application.

————, Title 5, Government organization and employees, Part III, Employees, Subpart G, Insurance and annuities, Chapter 81, Compensation for work injuries.

————, Title 7, Agriculture, Chapter 31, Rural electrification and telephone service, Subchapter IV, Rural Telephone Bank, Section 947, Borrowing power, telephone debentures, issuance, interest rates, terms and conditions, ratio to paid-in capital and retained earnings, investments in debentures, debentures as security, purchase and sale of debentures by the Secretary of the Treasury, treatment as public debt transactions of the United States, exclusion of transactions from budget totals.

————, Title 16, Conservation, Chapter 12A, Tennessee Valley Authority.

————, Title 29, Labor, Chapter 18, Employee retirement income security program, Subchapter III, Plan termination insurance, Subtitle A, Pension benefit guaranty corporation, Section 1305, Pension benefit guaranty funds.

————, Title 31, Money and finance, Subtitle II, The budget process, Chapter 11, The budget and fiscal, budget, and program information, Section 1105, Budget contents and submission to Congress.

————, Title 31, Money and finance, Subtitle VI, Miscellaneous, Chapter 91, Government corporations.

————, Title 33, Navigation and navigable waters, Chapter 26, Water pollution prevention and control, Subchapter I, Research and related programs, Section 1251, Congressional declaration of goals and policy. As of April 24, 2012:
http://epw.senate.gov/water.pdf

————, Title 41, Public contracts, Subtitle I, Federal procurement policy, Division C, Procurement, Chapter 45, Contract financing, Section 4504, Conditions for progress payments.

————, Title 42, The public health and welfare, Chapter 55, National environmental policy, Section 4321, Congressional declaration and purpose.

————, Title 42, The public health and welfare, Chapter 82, Solid waste disposal, Subchapter I, General provisions, Section 6901, Congressional findings.

————, Title 42, The public health and welfare, Chapter 85, Air pollution prevention and control. As of April 24, 2012:
http://www.gpo.gov/fdsys/pkg/USCODE-2008-title42/pdf/USCODE-2008-title42-chap85.pdf

U.S. Constitution, Article I, Legislative department, Section 8, Clause 18, All necessary and proper laws.

U.S. Department of Energy, "Calendar Year Reports," undated. As of April 23, 2012:
http://energy.gov/ig/calendar-year-reports

————, Office of Civilian Radioactive Waste Management, *Alternative Means of Financing and Managing the Civilian Radioactive Waste Management Program*, Washington, D.C., DOE/RW-0546, August 2001. As of April 23, 2012:
http://brc.gov/sites/default/files/documents/amfm_report_2001.pdf

————, Office of Audit Services, *The Office of Civilian Radioactive Waste Management's Corrective Action Program*, Washington, D.C., DOE/IG-0736, August 2006. As of April 23, 2012:
http://energy.gov/ig/downloads/office-civilian-radioactive-waste-managements-corrective-action-program-doeig-0736

————, "Secretary Chu Announces Blue Ribbon Commission on America's Nuclear Future," press release, January 29, 2010a. As of April 23, 2012:
http://energy.gov/articles/secretary-chu-announces-blue-ribbon-commission-americas-nuclear-future

————, Office of Chief Financial Officer, *FY 2011 Congressional Budget Request*, Vol. 6, February 2010b.

USEC—*See* U.S. Enrichment Corporation.

U.S. Enrichment Corporation, "History," undated. As of April 19, 2012:
http://www.usec.com/company/history

U.S. Environmental Protection Agency, "Yucca Mountain Standards," last updated July 8, 2011. As of April 23, 2012:
http://www.epa.gov/rpdweb00/yucca/

U.S. General Accounting Office, *Nuclear Waste: Quarterly Report as of March 31, 1989—Report to Congressional Requesters*, Washington, D.C., GAO/RCED-89-178, August 1989.

————, *Nuclear Waste: Yucca Mountain Project Behind Schedule and Facing Major Scientific Uncertainties—Report to the Chairman, Subcommittee on Clean Air and Nuclear Regulation, Senate Committee on Environment and Public Works*, Washington, D.C., GAO/RCED-93-124, May 1993.

————, *Nuclear Waste: Comprehensive Review of the Disposal Program Is Needed—Report to the Congress*, Washington, D.C., GAO/RCED-94-299, September 1994a.

————, *Nuclear Waste: DOE's Management and Organization of the Nevada Repository Project—Report to the Chairman, Subcommittee on Investigations and Oversight, Committee on Science, Space, and Technology, House of Representatives*, Washington, D.C., GAO/RCED-95-27, December 1994b.

————, *Government Corporations: Profiles of Existing Government Corporations—Report to the Ranking Minority Member, Subcommittee on Post Office and Civil Service, Committee on Governmental Affairs, U.S. Senate*, Washington, D.C., GAO/GGD-96-14, December 1995. As of April 19, 2012:
http://purl.access.gpo.gov/GPO/LPS21113

————, *Bonneville Power Administration: Better Management of BPA's Obligation to Provide Power Is Needed to Control Future Costs—Report to the Subcommittee on Energy and Water Development, Committee on Appropriations, House of Representatives*, Washington, D.C., GAO-04-694, July 2004. As of April 23, 2012:
http://purl.access.gpo.gov/GPO/LPS53896

————, *Principles of Federal Appropriations Law, Third Edition*, Volume III, Washington, D.C., GAO-08-978SP, 2008. As of April 26, 2012:
http://www.gao.gov/products/GAO-08-978SP

U.S. Government Accountability Office, homepage, undated. As of April 23, 2012:
http://www.gao.gov

————, *Federally Created Entities: An Overview of Key Attributes—Report to the Ranking Member, Committee on Finance, U.S. Senate*, Washington, D.C., GAO-10-97, October 2009. As of April 23, 2012:
http://purl.access.gpo.gov/GPO/LPS120056

————, *Effects of a Termination of the Yucca Mountain Repository Program and Lessons Learned*, GAO-11-229, Washington, D.C., April 8, 2011. As of April 19, 2012:
http://www.gao.gov/products/GAO-11-229

U.S. Nuclear Waste Technical Review Board, *Survey of National Programs for Managing High-Level Radioactive Waste and Spent Nuclear Fuel*, Arlington, Va., October 2009. As of April 19, 2012:
http://purl.access.gpo.gov/GPO/LPS118195

————, *Experience Gained from Programs to Manage High-Level Radioactive Waste and Spent Nuclear Fuel in the United States and Other Countries*, Arlington, Va., April 2011. As of April 19, 2012:
http://purl.fdlp.gov/GPO/gpo13663

U.S. Senate Committee on Energy and Natural Resources, "Jurisdiction," undated. As of April 19, 2012:
http://www.energy.senate.gov/public/index.cfm/jurisdiction

U.S. Statutes, Title 49, Section 863, Federal Power Act, August 26, 1935.

————, Title 50, Section 731, Bonneville Project Act, August 20, 1937.

————, Title 62, Section 982, Federal Tort Claims Act, June 25, 1948.

Verkuil, Paul R., "The Purposes and Limits of Independent Agencies," *Duke Law Journal*, Vol. 1988, No. 2–3, April–June 1988, pp. 257–279.

World Nuclear Association, "National Policies of Radioactive Waste Management—Appendix 3," undated. As of May 2, 2012:
http://www.world-nuclear.org/info/inf04ap3.html

Wright, Stephen J., administrator, Bonneville Power Administration, U.S. Department of Energy, statement before the Subcommittee on Water and Power, Committee on Natural Resources, U.S. House of Representatives, March 20, 2012. As of April 19, 2012:
http://energy.gov/sites/prod/files/3-20-12_Wright_BPA_FT_0.pdf